LOTS OF HOPE . . .

"There never was a night or a problem
That could defeat sunrise or hope."
—WILLIAM SLOANE COFFIN

To Bev, Sean, Joanie, Isabella and Cameron...
With Lots of Hope for the Wilburn Clan!

LOTS OF HOPE...

GARY ALAN WILBURN

PROGRESSIVEPUB

Stamford, CT

ISBN: 978-0-9701374-2-5

ProgressivePub
Stamford, CT
For information, email contactus@ProgressivePub.com

Cover art featuring Joanie and Isabella Wilburn
by Sean Wilburn and Kent LaGree,
sean@wilburnconsulting.com

Back cover photo of Gary A. Wilburn by Peter Hanson

Book design by Cheryl Mirkin,
CMF Graphic Design

Printed in the United States of America.

CONTENTS

ACKNOWLEDGEMENTS

I wish to thank my publisher Meyrick Payne of ProgressivePub,
my copyeditor Gail Linstrom, and my graphic designer
Cheryl Mirkin of CMF Graphic Design.

FORWARD

"The World is full of suffering.
It is also full of overcoming it."
—HELEN KELLER

"Faith is the assurance of things hoped for,
the conviction of things not seen."
—HEBREWS 1:11

"Hope arouses, as nothing else can, a passion for the possible."
—WILLIAM SLOANE COFFIN

This book is my second in a Trilogy on Faith, Hope and Love. My most recent book, *The God I Don't Believe In: Charting a New Course for Christianity,*[1] focused on the first of these timeless virtues: FAITH. This volume examines the second grand virtue: HOPE. The final volume will emphasize the third and greatest of them all: LOVE.

A year and a half ago, I was diagnosed most unexpectedly as having Amyotrophic Lateral Sclerosis (ALS), or Lou Gehrig's Disease. ALS is a progressive disease that attacks the body's motor neurons, leading to loss of muscle control, paralysis, and untimely death. Typically, ALS patients live one to five years after diagnosis. At present, there is still no known cause nor cure for this disease. But this is not the end of the story . . . this is the beginning of the cure. As Bertrand Russell wrote in his *Unpopular Essays,* "Extreme hopes are born of extreme misery."

When Bev and I first heard my diagnosis of ALS from my physician, Dr. Hiroshi Mitsumoto (Director of the Eleanor & Lou Gehrig

MDA/ALS Research Center at Columbia University, New York City), we were stunned and terrified. We had seen the movies and heard the stories of otherwise healthy and happy individuals who had struggled with this devastating disease and their untimely deaths. After nearly 40 years of our own marriage, after performing the marriage of our son to his lovely wife, Joanie, and watching them raise our two wonderful granddaughters, Isabella and Cameron, and after decades of leading several large congregations of hundreds of loving friends on the East and West Coasts, we were forced to leave the public ministry and start out on a new life on Christmas Eve, 2007.

Soon after we relocated to La Mision, a small beach community in Baja, CA, I was accepted into a selective 100-person, 12-month national clinical trial in San Francisco, testing a Synapse Diaphragm Conditioning System. As hopeful as that surgery and the subsequent studies were, the final result was that while the implant was FDA-approved for select spinal cord injuries, it did not work for me and other ALS patients as we had hoped.

As other new vistas of potential healing opened up, I eagerly stepped up to the plate. The day I began my clinical trial, an Italian newspaper reported successes with Lithium in slowing ALS. So I began a daily regimen of Lithium and other medicines. The same is true for treatment of Lyme Disease, which I had contracted in Connecticut. Since then I have been through several attempts at "de-toxing" my system of ALS-supportive elements, dietary restrictions, and even a series of treatments in a "Life Vessel." Still, to no avail. The ALS continues to progress. I have lost much of my voice (alas, no more preaching), and substantial muscle control in my legs, my upper body, and my breathing. As I write this I am grateful to be using an electric "Power Chair," a walker, an All-Terrain Vehicle (ATV), a breathing tube, a breathing-assist machine, and a voice-amplifier. Who knows what support technology I will need in the months to come.

But as my new friend, Dr. Alan Russell, Director of The McGowan Institute for Regenerative Medicine at Pittsburgh University, tells me: "Never give up hope. There is so much new research being done around the world that a breakthrough can always be just around the corner."

For now, my efforts are focused on the new frontiers of stem cell replacement. I believe that while death is a part of life, the God of Life wishes life to continue . . . if not in one form, then in another. Time is not on my side. But hope is. I have no fear of what ultimately lies ahead. We come from God and return to God. Life is changed, not taken away. But while I do not know what the future holds, as the old gospel hymn puts it, "I know whom I have believed, and am persuaded that [God] is able to keep that which I've committed unto [God] against that day." I believe in living each day fully, and am attempting to practice this in the face of increasing obstacles. My daily challenge is to continue to take responsibility for that over which I have control, to let go of my need to manage what I cannot control, and to live my life fully and productively in the moment.

Dum Spiro, Spero ("While I Breathe, I Hope."—Latin). Medical science is just beginning to uncover the mystery of how ALS works and how to cure it. Every day there is some new discovery or insight. "Hope is tenacious," says Paul Laurence Dunbar in his book, *The Strength of Gideon*. "It goes on living and working when science has dealt it what should be its deathblow."

Hopefully in the not-too-distant future, it will be possible to treat ALS patients like myself with stem-cell-based treatments created from an individual's own healthy cells. However, the only effective treatment at present is to use life to prolong life. Use of stem cells, while controversial, is an incredible discovery which someday in the near future will be used to save thousands of lives. This is consistent with my theology as a "Christian Panentheist," one who believes that not only is God outside of us, but that God is within us, interwoven into every fiber of our being, and interweaving us into everything else that exists. God is not "out there" somewhere; God is "in here" with us, in the makeup of every cell, every motor neuron, every thought, every emotion. Everything is in God and God is in everything. So in our quest for scientific and medical truth, we enter more fully into the Mystery we call God.

As Christopher Reeve (affectionately known by millions as "Superman"), who suffered from paralysis following a spinal cord injury which produced many symptoms similar to those of ALS, put it so passionately from his wheelchair while giving testimony in support of stem-cell research before Congress: "Is it more unethical for a woman to donate unused embryos that will never become human beings, or to let them be tossed away as so much garbage when they could help save thousands of lives? . . . Once you choose hope, anything is possible."[2]

Toward the end of his life, Christopher said, *"When John F. Kennedy promised that by the end of the 1960's we would put a man on the moon, everybody, including the scientists, shook their heads in dismay. But we did it! We can cure spinal-cord injuries too, if there is the will. What was possible in outer space is possible in inner space."* I believe that to be true today of ALS.

I believe in the power of Hope. Having been the minister of several large city churches in California and Connecticut, having been privileged to enter into the lives and hearts of hundreds of individuals of all colors and conditions of life, having performed hundreds of marriages and holy unions, and having delivered over one thousand sermons, lectures, and speeches over the past 40 years (all commentaries on the human condition and the divine alternatives), I am convinced that the great theologian, Reinhold Niebuhr, was right when he said that "nothing worth doing is completed in our lifetime, therefore we are saved by hope."

This book touches that raw nerve of hope in the personal stories of real people facing personal despair and in the national quandary of well-meaning leaders attempting to make the right decisions for a hopeful future for the earth.

"We must accept finite disappointment, but we must never lose infinite hope . . . If you lose hope," said Martin Luther King, Jr., "somehow you lose the vitality that keeps life moving, you lose that courage to be, that quality that helps you go on in spite of it all. And so today, I still have a dream."

Today I still have that dream. And I hope to share that dream with you in this volume. I have separated my thoughts on hope into three sections: "Hope for the Human Heart," "Hope for America's Soul," and "Hope for Life." Hope is not just a personal virtue; hope is a universal life-giving principle, a driving force for good, and a national imperative.

As President Barack Obama puts it, "Hope . . . Hope in the face of difficulty . . . Hope in the face of uncertainty! The audacity of hope! In the end, that is God's greatest gift to us, the bedrock of this nation. A belief in things not seen. A belief that there are better days ahead. . . . Hope is what led a band of colonists to rise up against an empire; what led the greatest of generations to free a continent and heal a nation; what led young women and young men to sit at lunch counters and brave fire hoses and march through Selma and Montgomery for freedom's cause. Hope is what led me here today—with a father from Kenya, a mother from Kansas; and a story that could only happen in the United States of America. Hope is the bedrock of this nation; the belief that our destiny will not be written for us, but by us; by all those men and women who are not content to settle for the world as it is; who have courage to remake the world as it should be."[3]

That challenge of remaking the world has fallen to you and me. And so I invite you to join me on this adventure of hope. Let it not be said of us that we retreated because of the enormity of the obstacles in front of us, or because of the failures of a misdirected past. One of the easiest things to do is to seek refuge in cynicism. Rather, let it be said of us that we assisted God in ushering in a new day of hope—for our personal lives, our families, our communities, our churches, synagogues and mosques, our schools and businesses . . . our nation . . . our world . . . and our very planet.

LOTS OF HOPE . . .
Gary

Gary can be reached at Gary@ProgressivePub.com.

HOPE FOR
THE HUMAN
HEART...

"Three grand essentials to happiness in this life are something to do, something to love, and something to hope for."
—JOSEPH ADDISON, ENGLISH POLITICIAN AND WRITER

Hope means to keep living
Amid desperation
And to keep humming
In the darkness.
Hoping is knowing that there is love,
It is trust in tomorrow,
It is falling asleep
And waking again
When the sun rises.
In the midst of a gale at sea,
It is to discover land.
In the eyes of another
It is to see that he understands you.
As long as there is still hope
There will also be prayer
And God will be holding you
In his hands.
—ANONYMOUS POET QUOTED BY DUTCH PRIEST,
PROFESSOR, AND PASTOR, HENRI J. M. NOUWEN

"In the midst of winter,
I found there was, within me, an invincible summer."
—ALBERT CAMUS, FRENCH EXISTENTIALIST WRITER

"They say that they built the train tracks over the
Alps between Venice and Vienna before there was
a train that could make the trip. They built it anyway . . .
. . . because they knew the train would come."
(FRANCIS MAYES, UNDER THE TUSCAN SUN)

CHAPTER 1

UNDIMMED BY HUMAN TEARS

"For surely I know the plans I have for you,
says the Lord,
plans for your welfare and not for harm,
to give you a future with hope."
—JEREMIAH 29:11

Those of you who are Garrison Keillor fans, as are my wife Bev and I, know about that fabled town of Lake Woebegone, Minnesota, "where all the women are strong, all the men are good looking, and all the children are above average."

In one of his stories of Lake Woebegone, Keillor tells about an old phone booth standing on the corner in the middle of town which had deteriorated over the years. The phone booth stood there, ramshackled, door hanging off of it, dirty with dust and cobwebs, but still the phone worked. No one ever used the phone to call out; they only answered it.

Time after time, when townspeople would pass by that old phone booth, mysteriously it would ring. There being no one else around, they would step into the booth and answer the phone. A voice coming from God-knows-where would comment on their personal appearance or would talk about the weather, or the vehicles and animals on the street, or would tell the person in the phone booth that their plaid pants didn't go with their striped coat.

One time when Garrison was walking by that spot in the center of town, the phone rang . . . persistently. So he went into the booth, looked around, and answered it. He was down that day – discouraged and dejected. Life seemed hopeless. He had been look-ing at the dirt and shuffling, rather than walking with his head aright. He couldn't bring himself to face the glory of the day because he was crestfallen. When he picked up the receiver and quietly said, "Hello," the voice said to him. "Cheer up. It's not that bad . . . and you're not the only one!"

God speaks to us in all sorts of ways. But the message is always the same. And what goes deepest to the heart goes widest to the world.

Clearly, at this crisis point in history, "HOPE" is one of the major rallying cries of America and the world. As the great Jewish theologian Abraham Heschel once said, "We live not by deeds alone, but by hopes for that which we do not even know how to utter. A person is what he hopes for." And I would add, a nation is what it hopes for . . . a government is what it hopes for . . . a community is what it hopes for . . . a humanity is what it hopes for.

Hope is not the same as optimism. Some people seem to be born optimists. They are always happy. Regardless of the circumstance, they always see the glass half-full. They always look for the cloud's silver lining, or the end of the rainbow, or the horse in the next room.

But hope is a different thing altogether than a positive attitude.

Vaclav Havel, the former president of Czechoslovakia, said this about hope: "I am not an optimist because I am not sure that everything ends well, nor am I a pessimist because I am so sure that everything ends badly. I just carry hope in my heart."

"Cheer up. It's not that bad . . . and you're not the only one."

Alexander Solzhenitsyn found that same experience in the prison cells of Soviet Russia: "In agonizing moments in camps," he wrote, "in columns of prisoners at night, in the freezing darkness through which the lanterns shone, there often arose in our throats something we wanted to shout out to the whole world, if only the world could have heard one of us."[4]

"And it was only when I lay there on rotting prison straw that I sensed within myself the first stirrings of good. Gradually it was disclosed to me that the line separating good and evil passes not through states, nor between classes, nor between political parties either – but right through every human heart – and through all human hearts. . . . All the writers who wrote about prison but did not themselves serve time there considered it their duty to express sympathy for prisoners and to curse prison. I . . . have served enough time there. I nourished my soul there, and I say without hesitation: 'Bless you, prison, for having been in my life.'"[5]

That is true Biblical Hope.

That kind of hope has nothing to do with optimism or circumstances. In fact, the opposite of hope is not pessimism but despair. Hope and despair can arise from the same circumstance. "When tragedy strikes, when trouble comes, when life disappoints us, we stand at the crossroads between hope and despair, torn and hurting. Despair cements us in the present; hope sends us dancing around dark corners trusting in a tomorrow we cannot see. Despair says that there is no place to go but here. Hope says that God is waiting for us someplace else. So begin again."[6]

"Cheer up. It's not that bad . . . and you're not the only one."

Christian hope carries this even further. "Christian hope is the power of resurrection from life's failures and defeats. It is the power of life's rebirth out of the shadows of earth."[7] It is Christian because it is grounded in the spirit of One who was betrayed, tortured, and forsaken, only to be raised from the dead. Our life began in his death. But the same God who raised Jesus from the dead continues to raise all people of hope, whatever their religion, or lack of it, from the tombs of their resentment and despair. Hope gives us the strength to get up again. Hopeful people are eternal beginners.

"Through the power of hope we don't give up and we don't give ourselves up. . . . the Christian hope's proclamation of God is subversive talk of God. 'Other lords and powers rule over us, but in You alone do we hope,' cried the Jewish prophet Isaiah."[8] The same is true for the followers of the Islamic prophet Mohammed, and of every other religion of peace.

In our respectable and conformist Christianity, which we often identify with the state or the "good life," this subversive talk about God has become strange and alien. We do not understand the book of Revelation because we do not understand the martyrs. But Christians who are living under persecution, and Christians who are working against injustice and violence in their own democratic countries, understand its language very well. "Ascetic Christianity called the world evil and left it. Humanity is waiting for a revolutionary Christianity which will call the world evil and change it" (Walter Rauschenbusch).

As Senator Robert Kennedy said in his address at the University of Capetown, South Africa, "It is from numberless diverse acts of courage and belief that human history is shaped. Each time a man stands up for an ideal, or acts to improve the lot of others, or strikes out against injustice, he sends forth a tiny ripple of hope, and crossing each other from a million different centers of energy and daring those ripples build a current which can sweep down the mightiest walls of oppression and resistance."[9]

"It is hope at work," as Tom Stella reminds us, "when a woman, despite her fear and insecurity, re-enters the workforce after years spent raising her family. It is hope enfleshed when a man with a terminal diagnosis refuses to give up on life but instead continues, without denial of his circumstance, to purse his goals with all the energy he can muster. And it is hope when a person carrying the wounds of a relationship gone sour chooses to become vulnerable again for the sake of living life to the full. Hope is not wishing things were different; it is choosing to make the most of our lives given the given . . . "[10]

It was raw hope and courage on the field that awesome day a few years ago at the Seattle Special Olympics, when those nine brave contestants, all physically or mentally challenged, assembled at the starting line for the 100-yard dash. At the gunshot each of them started out, not exactly in a dash, but with a relish to run the race to the finish and win. All, that is, except one little boy who stumbled on the asphalt, tumbled over a couple of times, and began to cry.

The other eight heard the boy cry. They slowed down and looked back. Then they all turned around and went back . . . every one of the competitors. One girl with Down's Syndrome bent down and kissed him and said, "This will make it better." They reached down and picked their friend up off the ground. Then all nine of them linked arms and walked together to the finish line.

They didn't win the race, but they won the victory. Everyone in that stadium stood and cheered and applauded, and the cheering went on and on for several minutes—as it does at every Special Olympics. People who were there that day are still telling the story. Why? Because deep down we know this one thing: What matters most in this life is more than winning for ourselves. What matters in this life is helping others win, even if it means slowing down and changing our course.

Having hope doesn't make it better—
it makes us want to make it better!
"Cheer up. It's not that bad . . .
and you're not the only one."

Thanks be to God. Amen.

CHAPTER 2

TAKE COURAGE

Lewis Carroll, the English writer of Alice in Wonderland, once told a friend, "I'm very brave generally . . . only today I happen to have a headache!" How easy it is to mistake bravado for bravery . . . comfort for well-being.

"'Tis the business of little minds to shrink," wrote Thomas Paine, "but he whose heart is firm, and whose conscience approves his conduct, will pursue his principles unto death."[11]

When the center of our life is destroyed, when that which we most treasure, our very reason for living, is taken from us . . . how do we respond? Do we cower in fear or do we take courage? As Mark Twain put it, "Courage is the art of being the only one who knows you're scared to death!"

In Hebrew the word for courage is *ometz lev*, or literally, "strength of heart." Courage, "inner strength," is not something we work up by our own willpower and determination. Courage is something that is given us to be shared. A soldier is "given heart" by his comrades to face the enemy. In the face of persecution and uncertainty, people share and give each other "courage-ment," the "heart to resist."

"Faith and courage are partners. Courage gives faith the strength to question, to remain faithful in the midst of doubt, to embrace a mystery that confounds all our easy answers and certainties. Faith gives courage the strength to risk intimacy, the vigor to be humble and vulnerable, and the confidence to be compassionate. . . .

"[But] when faith and courage are divorced, courage loses its dynamic character; it stagnates into false bravado or paralyzing fear and, not surprisingly, its companion—faith—is transformed into either idolatrous certainty or deadening doubt."[12]

Life shrinks or expands in proportion to one's courage.

Most of us have a collection of favorite stories with which we have grown up. These stories of past courage, as John F. Kennedy reminds us in his *Profiles of Courage*, can teach; they can offer hope; they can provide inspiration. But they cannot supply courage itself. For this each person must look into his own soul.

Don Quixote de la Mancha knew the power of faith to fuel one's courage:

"One man scorned and covered with scars
still strove with his last ounce of courage
to reach the unreachable stars;
and the world was better for this."

"It is curious . . .," wrote Mark Twain, "curious that physical courage should be so common in the world, and moral courage so rare."

Several years ago, Archbishop Desmond Tutu was in New York City to receive the prized "Union Medal" from the Union Theological Seminary. Few human beings in our lifetime know the deep meaning of "courage" as viscerally as does Desmund Tutu, having witnessed for decades the horrors of abuse and death of his own people. "If we take the incarnation seriously," Tutu said, "we must be concerned about where people live, how they live, whether they have justice, whether they are uprooted and dumped as rubbish in resettlement camps, whether they are detained without trial, whether they receive an inferior education, whether they have a say in the decisions that affect their lives most deeply."

"Not everything that is faced can be changed," James Baldwin reminds us, "but nothing can be changed until it is faced."

You cannot discover new oceans unless you have the courage to lose sight of the shore. "The greatest test of courage on earth is to bear defeat without losing heart."

"Security is mostly superstition," said Helen Keller. "It does not exist in nature, nor do the children of men as a whole experience it. Avoiding danger is no safer in the long run than outright exposure. Life is either a daring adventure, or nothing. To keep our faces toward change and behave like free spirits in the presence of fate is strength undefeatable."

"Courage is a crucial virtue," as Bill Coffin reminded us, "for once again the currents of history are churning into rapids, threatening to carry before them everything we have loved, trusted, looked to for pleasure and support. We are being called upon to live with enormous insecurity. [Our] churches could become centers of creative and courageous thinking. [Or] they could become sanctuaries for frightened Americans, recruiting grounds for authoritarian figures and movements, some of which already bear the earmarks of an emerging fascism.

"Will we be scared to death or scared to life? It all depends on where we find our ultimate security."[13]

A while back I had the privilege of addressing some of New Canaan, Connecticut's best "encouragers," our Volunteer Fire Company, at their Annual Awards Dinner. Those courageous fire-fighters knew the reality of what I was talking about when I reminded them that one of the best definitions of a "hero" is simply a man or woman who chooses to remain in the fire one minute longer than everyone else.

In fact, the only kind of courage that matters is the kind that gets you from one moment to the next. Start doing the things you think should be done, and start being what you think society should become . . .

Do you believe in free speech? Then speak freely.

Do you love the truth? Then tell it.

Do you believe in an open society? Then act in the open.

Do you believe in a decent and humane society? Then behave decently and humanely.

"Take Courage," my friends. No one knows what the next day might hold. Each of us, together with the Eternal, are all that any of us has to count on. And all of us, together with one another, are all that God has to count on.

And remember, as Noam Chomsky used to say, "If you are not offending people who ought to be offended, you're doing something wrong."

> *God of the coming years, through paths unknown*
> *We follow thee.*
> *When we are strong, Lord, leave us not alone;*
> *Our refuge be.*
> *Be thou for us in life our daily bread,*
> *Our heart's true home when all our years have sped.*[14]

CHAPTER 3

LIVING ABOVE
OUR CIRCUMSTANCES

I asked a friend recently, "How are you doing these days?" She answered, "O.K. I guess, under the circumstances." How often have you and I said the same thing?

"Under the Circumstances." That's our basic problem. There are too many people who live every day of their lives "under the circumstances." They never allow themselves to get too hopeful or too passionate about anything for fear that they might fail at it; they never hold their head up high in a crowd because they fear someone will knock it off; and they never dream about a better day because they are fearful it will never come; they never invest too much hope in things becoming different.

What a waste! To have the whole world awaiting our active participation in its renewal . . . while we remain tied down by our own dreary perception that we could never make a difference anyway.

The Apostle Paul, no stranger to adversity, said it best, "I can do all things through Christ who strengtheneth me." With a God who is waiting to recreate the world through us, how could any of us claim that we are fated to live "under the circumstances"?

Clara Lemlich was a small woman, no more than five feet tall, but solidly built. She looked like a teenager, with her soft round face and blazing eyes, 'though she was only nineteen. Clara was headed downtown that day, through the crowded, teeming immigrant precincts of the Lower East Side of Manhattan. She couldn't have known it at the time, but her one small act of defiance was about to galvanize a generation of oppressed women.

Clara's father was a deeply religious man, one of about three thousand Jews in the Ukrainian trading town of Gorodok. He spent long days in prayer and studying Torah. Clara was expected to provide for the family while her father and brothers studied the Scriptures. In 1903 she and her family had joined the flood of two million Eastern European Jewish immigrants that entered the United States "yearning to be free."

Six years later, in the fall of 1909, nineteen-year-old Clara stood in the large crowd of factory shirtwaist blouse-makers, where she worked, listening to men give long speeches cautioning against striking. The women had gathered to bemoan their circumstances:

- their 60-80 hour, 7-day a week labor,
- their $6-a-week salaries,
- their having to bring their own materials and equipment,
- their hazardous and infectious working conditions,
- their being marched every few hours in groups to filthy toilets by their male foreman who had the keys, and
- their prison-like, full-body searches by male guards at the exit door.

After over two hours of male speeches, this "thin wisp of a girl" asked to speak. As she stepped onto the platform, the crowd quieted. Everyone knew Clara Lemlich, the brave factory worker with two broken ribs who had just been released from the hospital after having been savagely beaten by management-hired thugs for her union involvement. Her words, spoken in clear and passionate Yiddish, echoed through the hall. It was a clarion call to action.

"I have listened to all the speakers," she said, "and I have no further patience for talk. I am a working girl, one of those striking against intolerable conditions. I am one of those who feels and suffers from the things pictured. . . . I offer a resolution that a general strike be declared—now!" The audience rose to their feet in wild applause and cheered.

The next morning, throughout New York's garment district, over 15,000 waistmakers walked out. Police officers began arresting strikers, as judges fined them and consigned some to labor camps. One judge, while sentencing a picketer for "incitement," roared, "You are striking blows against God and Nature whose law is that man shall earn his pay by the sweat of his brow. You are on strike against God!"

That brave struggle of Clara Lemlich and those other women workers would become known as "The Uprising of the Twenty Thousand." When it was over, the strikers won a shorter workweek of only 52 hours, a slight pay increase, and the end of unfair paycheck deductions for supplies, chairs, and lockers.

Clara Lemlich was blacklisted by the powerful Garment Association, but hailed for her passionate bravery by millions of women around the world who would come to follow her example. I have to believe that her father's Yiddish prayers for the re-creation of the world were answered.

As Abraham Lincoln put it, "To sin by silence when they should protest, makes cowards of human beings."

Clara Lemlick chose to live above her circumstances.

Just over fifty years ago, young Rosa Parks made a simple decision that sparked a world-wide revolution. When a white man demanded she give up her seat on a Montgomery public bus, the simple seamstress said "NO!"

It was an understood law, and it had worked so well for so long. The front sections of all public buses were reserved for the deserving—only white people were valuable enough to sit there. Non-whites (that is to say blacks or colored) were required to board the bus at the front, pay the driver, then exit the bus, walk around to the back door, climb aboard, and sit in the rear seats.

Rosa paid her fare that day and chose to walk down the aisle to the center of the bus and sit down. An angry white man demanded that she give up her seat and move to the back. But she would not stand for it. She had lived too much of her life "under the circumstances" . . . and it was to end right then and there.

The moment when Rosa Parks refused to get up, an entire race of people began to stand up for their rights as human beings. It was a simple act that took extraordinary courage in Montgomery, Alabama, in 1955. It was a place where black people had no rights which white people had to respect. It was a time when racial discrimination was so common that many blacks never questioned it.

At least not out loud.

But then came Rosa Parks . . . and Jim Crow laws had met their match.

Rosa's refusal infused 50,000 blacks in Montgomery with the will to walk [for miles] rather than risk daily humiliation on the city's buses."[15]

Her arrest led to an unprecedented display of black unity in the United States that has not been witnessed since. Black people stayed off Montgomery's city buses for a year, until the U.S. Supreme Court ruled the segregated busing policy was illegal. They were inspired to stay off those buses at Sunday church services and Wednesday prayer meetings, where their aching souls were soothed by freedom songs, and their aching feet swayed by stirring sermons.

"This gentle giant, whose quietness belied her toughness, became the catalyst for a movement that broke the back of legalized segregation in the United States, gave rise to the astounding leadership of Dr. Martin Luther King, Jr., and inspired fighters for freedom and justice throughout the world. . . .

In one of her last interviews . . . Rosa spoke of what she would like people to say about her after she passed away:

> "I'd like people to say I'm a person who always wanted to be free and wanted it not only for myself; freedom is for all human beings". . . It was a desire embedded in her by her grandfather. He taught his children and grandchildren not to put up with mistreatment. "It was passed down almost in our genes," she wrote. . . . "I remember that sometimes [my grandfather] would call white men by their first names, or their whole names, and not say, 'Mister.'
>
> "People always say that I didn't give-up my seat because I was tired, but that isn't true. I was not tired physically, or no more tired than I usually was at the end of a working day. . . . No, the only tired I was, was tired of giving in."[16]

When South African freedom icon Nelson Mandela came to Detroit in 1990, the person he was most honored to meet was Rosa Parks . . . he said that she was his inspiration and hope while he was in jail for 27 years, and it was her example that had inspired South African freedom fighters. Mandela called her "the David who challenged Goliath."

Poet Laureate Maya Angelou said of her, "Mrs. Parks is for me probably what the Statue of Liberty was for immigrants. She stood for the future, and a better future. She was as tender as a rose and she was as strong as steel."

"I am leaving this legacy to all of you," Rosa said, "to bring peace, justice, equality, love and a fulfillment of what our lives should be. Without vision, the people will perish, and without courage and inspiration, dreams will die—the dream of freedom and peace."

Rosa Parks could easily have chosen to continue "to live under the circumstances." But she refused. And the world is different today for her having done so.

"No one need be afraid of fear, only afraid that fear will stop him or her from doing what's right. Courage means being well aware of the worst that can happen, being scared almost to death, and then doing the right thing anyhow."[17]

There is no room for predestination in hopeful faith. The only predestination the Bible knows about is you and me being predestined to the divine work of redeeming, restoring, and mending the world.

Eleanor Roosevelt said it well, "No one can hurt you without your consent." And in the words of Mahatma Gandhi, "They cannot take away our self respect if we do not give it to them."

The world is waiting for a new breed of Clara Lemlicks and Rosa Parkses to rise up and challenge the status quo. It appalls me to see how widespread the practice of feigned impotence and buck-passing is in our society. You would think by reading the daily paper that in the youngest and most creative nation in the world, there is no way to solve the massive social problems of the day: endless killing, pandemic poverty, global environmental destruction, religious terror, unprecedented economic disparity, unacceptable educational blight, racial injustice, gender inequality, sexual hostility, rampant crime and addiction, and national political ideology driven by fear and intolerance. So, lacking the vigor to deal with big problems, we allow ourselves to become mesmerized by little ones.

I would challenge each of us to take responsibility for that over which we have control. Instead of blaming others, choose to live your own life responsibly. Instead of giving up because the load is too great, let us choose to make small commitments and keep them. Instead of criticizing others' failures, let us choose to be agents of light. "Better to light one candle that to curse the darkness."

When you make a mistake, correct it, learn from it—right then. When others let you down, find another way to accomplish your task. When you think you are not good enough or smart enough or skilled enough or educated enough or powerful enough to succeed, listen to the voice of God within you, not your grandparent's voice or your parent's voice. Listen to God. And step out in faith. One person plus God is a majority.

Rosa Parks had no control over the preceding generations of hatred, arrogance, and ignorance which kept her from sitting in the front of that bus. She couldn't vote. She couldn't use the nearest bathroom or drink from the clean fountain. She couldn't sit at a counter in a diner. She couldn't walk into a white school or call for a policeman. But she did what she could. SHE JUST SAID, "NO". And, by God, she wasn't going to stand for it anymore. SO SHE SAT DOWN! And because one woman sat down on that Montgomery bus, millions of people around the world have stood up for what they believe.

Nearly 50 years before Rosa sat down on that bus, Theodore Roosevelt stood up and declared:

> It is not the critic who counts; not the man who points out how the strong man stumbles, or where the doer of deeds could have done them better. The credit belongs to the man who is actually in the arena, whose face is marred by dust and sweat and blood; who strives valiantly; who errs, and comes short again and again, because there is no effort without error and shortcoming; but who does actually strive to do the deeds; who knows the great enthusiasms, the great devotions; who spends himself in a worthy cause; who at the best knows in the end the triumph of high achievement, and who at the worst, if he fails, at least fails while daring greatly, so that his place

shall never be with those cold and timid souls who know neither victory nor defeat.

Oh, my friends . . . Our faith should quell our fears, [but]
never our courage.[18]

Doing all right under the circumstances? Well, get over it! Then
choose to *rise above* them.

And may God bless you as you dare to take your stand.

CHAPTER 4

TINY RIPPLES OF HOPE

I recently learned of a minister who was invited by a small inner-city church to be their guest preacher for Advent. Before the sermon, he invited the children to join him up front for a children's message. About ten children came forward. As he began to speak with them, he noticed that one little girl had brought something with her. She was holding it in such a way that it caught his attention, and so he asked her,

"Jamel, is that an Easter basket?"

"Yes," she replied.

"Well, it sure is pretty," the minister said. "But this is the time of year we like to talk about the Coming of Jesus."

"I know that," she said. "That's why I brought my Easter basket. That's what Mary did in the Bible story. She didn't have much either. But the angel told her that her that because of Jesus Coming, her basket would be filled with good things!"

"Every Christmas I'm struck at how the word of the Lord hits the world with the force of a hint. We want God to be God, and God wants to be a babe in a manger." [19]

Harriet Beecher Stow, the Litchfield, Connecticut, author of *Uncle Tom's Cabin*, also wrote *Christmas or The Good Fairy*. It is a story about a young woman, Ellen Stuart, who is in a quandary about what to give her friends for Christmas. They all are well off, have everything, and are "sick and tired of what they've got!" as she puts it.

Ellen's aunt leads her to a window at the back of their big house, which looks across an alley to a row of poor shanties. "What do you see?" the aunt asks her. Apparently for the first time, Ellen sees the needs of the world literally at her doorstep. She becomes a "good fairy," taking food, clothing, and other help to the people in the shanties. Her aunt reminds her that Jesus was born in a lowly manger and grew up to be a brother of the poor, lowly, outcast, and distressed.

She challenges those of us in "splendid dwellings" with "worlds of money," as she put it, to be more concerned with those on whom the Babe of Bethlehem focused.

But Ellen, like all of us, was a child of her times—which 150 years ago were more accustomed to indulging in a romanticized Christian sensibility. Tackling the big issues of the day, like poverty, was one of the marks of a cultured, compassionate human being.

What different times we live in today! "Mention poverty to just about anybody in just about any circle these days and very little of what you say after that will matter," said Bill Coffin. "People's attention tends to disengage when poverty is mentioned. It's one of these words that numb the mind."

As one columnist puts it, "I can't pinpoint exactly when poverty became yesterday's news. But somehow the plight of the poor was reduced to cold statistics and images of destitute homelessness. From there it was an easy step to irrelevance. We don't like to talk about poverty; it's indelicate, like talking about religion at a social gathering."[20]

It's sad, really, given that so much of Jesus' life, his conversations, his teachings, and his understanding and expression of the gospel have to do with relationships between the poor and the wealthy. In both cases, it is a matter of dignity: the dignity of those of little means, the dignity of hard work, the dignity of altruism, and the dignity of a society which organizes itself in a way that rewards all people for their service to the common good.

During these days of job losses and cutbacks, when we are reminded of the Almighty God coming to us in poverty, of "The God Who Needs Nothing" sharing the earth with us, and of the intention of that same God to "raise all ships" through a just and caring society, it should give us pause to realize that Jamel had it right with her Easter basket.

One of the world's finest theologians today is Jurgen Moltmann of the University of Tubingen in Germany. I spoke with him a couple of years ago at Yale University. Moltmann is convinced that our celebration of the Incarnation of God not only points backward to the first coming of Christ, but also forward to the second, providing Christians with a vision of the future. One of the evidences of that coming kingdom is the presence of humanizing conditions and relationships between people.

"The kingdom of God will be a kingdom of peace and justice," he says. "The call to anticipate that in our lives means to love and seek out others with whom we strive for human and civil rights based on the idea of a divinely-ordained human dignity. This will involve an accounting of the human costs of our economy and a just distribution of opportunities for work and profits."

Not long ago our House of Representatives passed the final and largest part of its $95 billion tax cuts. And, to be fair, it has been demonstrated that tax cuts can create the incentives for a more healthy economy. I think most of us would agree that reducing taxes on businesses often results in greater economic growth—and more jobs and employment mean more revenue which could be used for good causes.

But, here again, the issue is "who is most affected by these tax cuts—those with very little or those with quite a lot?" According to reports, the House budget intends to cut $51 billion over five years from proven social programs like Medicaid, food stamps for the poor, child-support enforcement, student loans, and the like. If we believe that one of the evidences of Hope is "the presence of humanizing conditions and relationships between people," then we need to ask, "Are the poor and vulnerable in a society the ones who should shoulder the lion's share of these cuts?"

The U.S. Budget is a great moral document of our values. It should be studied in our seminaries and classrooms. President George H. Bush promised that "the truly needy will have a safety net." That has yet to happen. We need to reassure that promise under this new administration of Barack Obama.

Churches in our day are a bit like families: they tend to be havens in a heartless world, but they reinforce that world by caring more for its victims than by challenging its assumptions. Christ wants us to challenge the assumptions of our nation, just as he challenged those of his.

I think it is a disgrace that charity should have to substitute for justice—that the churches of our country should be forced to bandage the wounds of our poorest citizens because our government can't be bothered. I believe that adequate food, housing, medical care, and education in this country are human rights, not a matter of optional charity. It is part of our social contract with one another.

AmeriCares' free clinics are helping. But volunteer nurses and doctors can't treat enough families. Churches and other nonprofits are helping. But we can't build enough Habitat houses, nor tutor enough schoolchildren, nor find enough Big Brothers and Big Sisters, nor go on enough mission trips, nor staff enough soup kitchens, nor fill enough Thanksgiving and Christmas grocery bags to fix poverty. And it is not the government's responsibility to pay for it all, either.

Tom Hunter is a 44-year-old Scottish-American businessman, who built a small sneaker business into a chain of 260 stores. A few months later, Tom decided to personally invest $100 million in projects to elevate Africans out of poverty. "We don't want to create a dependency culture in Africa," he said. "We make an investment. We want a return. We wouldn't just give the money and hope for the best. I am a Scotsman after all!"

Tom's plan is to bypass the usual channels of governmental and nongovernmental organization (NGO) development aid, and instead provide closely audited injections of cash to permit the poorest villagers to grow more abundant crops. He also plans to spend the money on health care, AIDS, and education in those villages to enable them to take the first step up on the rungs of self-development.

Tom calls his form of giving "Venture Philanthropy!" I love that! While another Scot, the great missionary David Livingston, invested his life in eliminating the slave trade in Africa during Victorian times, this modern Scot wants to eliminate Africa's slavery to poverty. [21]

The root causes of evil are not just individual, but social, and require a civilized people to be constantly vigilant in reforming the structures of society which kill life rather than give it. At the back end, the compassion of charity and rehabilitation is essential. At the front end, the compassion of social justice and communal dignity is equally essential.

In America we do social charity very well. But we are not so good with social justice. Charity is voluntary and optional. Social justice is part of our social contract with one another. We must never forget Thomas Jefferson's plea for America: "I tremble for my country when I recall that God is just."

At the conclusion of his Day of Affirmation Address at the University of Cape Town, South Africa, two years to the day before his assassination, Robert Kennedy spoke to thousands of students in the same spirit of the Prophet Isaiah:

"It is from the numberless diverse acts of courage and belief that human history is shaped. Each time a person stands up for an ideal, or acts to improve the lot of others, or strikes out against injustice, that person sends forth a tiny ripple of hope, and crossing each other from a million different centers of energy and daring, those ripples build a current which can sweep down the mightiest walls of oppression and resistance."

So let us work together, my friends, for a Hope-filled world. "With a good conscience our only sure reward, with history the final judge of our deeds, let us go forth to lead the land we love, asking His blessing and His help, but knowing that here on earth God's work must truly be our own."[22]

CHAPTER 5

WHATEVER HAPPENED TO JOHNNY?

J esus was a great storyteller. One of his best was the story of the
Good Samaritan. You remember it: Jesus was asked by a lawyer
what a person must do to inherit eternal life. Like the good Jew
that he was, Jesus answered the man's question with a question:
"What is written in the Law of Moses?" The man answered, "You
shall love the Lord your God with all your heart, and with all your
soul, and with all your strength, and with all your mind; and your
neighbor as yourself."

Jesus replied, "You have given the right answer; do this, and you
will live."

But, wanting to justify himself, he asked Jesus, "Who is my
neighbor?" To which Jesus replied with a story about a man who
was traveling the road from Jerusalem to Jericho and was attacked,
stripped, beaten, robbed, and left for dead by thieves. By chance a
priest came upon the scene and passed by the man on the other
side of the road. He did so as every religious Levite was required to
do, since his religious law stated, "touch not the unclean thing."
But when a Samaritan (the equivalent of an untouchable) came
along, he was moved with pity: He poured out his oil and wine on
the man's wounds, bandaged him with his own garment, sat him
upon his own animal, brought him to an inn, paid the innkeeper
in advance from his meager savings, and told him, "Please take care
of him and when I return I will reimburse you for your troubles."

Then Jesus asked the lawyer, "Which of these three do you think
was a neighbor to the man who fell into the hands of the robbers?"
He answered, "The one who showed him mercy." Then Jesus said
to him, "Go and do likewise." (Luke 10:25-37)

Every one of us has heard this story before. And we all know
what it means: help you neighbor. Right? So let's do a little exercise
in imagination. Suppose we enter the world of Jesus' parable in our
North American context.

"We, too, go down from Jerusalem to Jericho. We encounter a
woman who fell among thieves and, by grace, do not pass by on
the other side but greet her with compassion. The next week we
repeat the trip and encounter a similar victim whom we likewise

treat with compassion. Twice during the following month we have to make the trip (business is brisk just before the holiday season), and each time there is another victim to be treated.

"By now a thought has occurred to us: 'This is a stupid way to respond. We keep binding up victims every time we make the trip, but nothing changes. Binding up wounds isn't enough; we've got to ensure that people don't need to be bound up in the first place.'

"So next week at the town council the local selectman, responding to our phone calls, introduces preventative legislation: (1) nobody can make the trip alone, unless he or she is adequately armed and able to ward off attack; (2) the number of patrol cars on the road will be doubled as a message to potential brigands; and (3) no nighttime travel will be allowed until we pass a local bond issue to get better lighting, especially at the hairpin curve where four out of every five robberies occur.

"Such measures may make the road a little safer and virtually eliminate highway robberies and muggings, although the tax rate will soar. But the thieves, who are not stupid, will simply transfer their activities to areas more conducive to their personal health and longevity, and there will be a sudden rash of house-breakings in suburban Jericho.

"More radical steps are necessary ('radical' in the sense of getting to the 'radix,' or root, of the trouble). Those who want to meet the problem head-on will have to answer such questions as:

"Why do so many people steal in the first place?

"Is it because they can't get jobs? (There is a high correlation between upward rates of unemployment and upward rates of crime.)

"Do we provide so little good education for young people that they turn to beating up travelers out of frustration or boredom?

"Is there not a parent or guardian at home who knows who their children's friends are and where they are at all times?

"Is there even a home to go home to, or do the thieves live on the streets? Has anyone bothered to talk to people who live on the streets to find out?

"Have they never been taught right from wrong, or do they see themselves as modern day Robin Hoods?

"Are the thieves facing debts they can't pay off because interest rates are exorbitant?

"What percentage of the thieves are from minority groups—the last hired and the first fired—who thus have lots of time for moonlighting?

"Finally, and of most importance, 'Whose job is it to deal with these problems?'"[23]

Now, let's step back out of Jesus' parable. The fact is that the majority of poor people in America are not unemployed. They are underemployed. "The man who washes cars does not own one. The clerk who files cancelled checks at the bank has $2.02 in her own account. The woman who copy-edits medical textbooks has not been to a dentist in a decade.

"This is the forgotten America. At the bottom of its working world, millions live in the shadow of prosperity, in the twilight between poverty and well-being . . . They serve [us] Big Macs . . . They harvest [our] food, clean [our] offices, and sew [our] clothes. In a California factory, they package lights for [our] kids' bikes. In a New Hampshire plant, they assemble books of wallpaper samples to help [us] redecorate.

"They are shaped by their invisible hardships. Some are climbing out of welfare, drug addiction, or homelessness. Others have been trapped for life in a perilous zone of low-wage work. Some of their children are malnourished. Some have been sexually abused. Some live in crumbling housing that contributes to their children's asthma, which means days absent from school. Some of their youngsters do not even have the eyeglasses they need to see the chalkboard clearly. . . .

"An inconvenience to an affluent family—minor car trouble, a brief illness, disrupted child care—is a crisis to them, for it can threaten their ability to stay employed. They spend everything and save nothing. They are always behind on their bills. They have minuscule bank accounts or none at all, and so pay more fees and higher interest rates than more secure Americans."[24]

Let me tell you about a friend of mine. Johnny (his real name) showed up one day in the food line at our historic Gothic church in downtown Los Angeles. As we spoke together in line with 60-some daily guests, Johnny told me he was down on his luck and asked for money for a bus ticket to San Diego. Then he told me his story. It seems that he had been a college professor, a scientist probably, was extremely intelligent, had written a college textbook (which he later showed me), but had fallen on hard times. Because of some personal problems, his marriage fell apart; he was let go from the university; his family rejected him and forced him out of the house. (He might well have had a mental breakdown during this time.) Now he was disoriented, disheveled, broke, and homeless. But not dumb! Johnny learned quickly that sleeping while guarding his few possessions on a five-hour bus ride to San Diego at night was safer, quieter, and cheaper than a room in bad areas of downtown L.A.!

I learned back then that it only takes six weeks for a fully-functioning person to move from employment and housing to poverty and the street. When your income source dries up, you have to evacuate your residence and often relocate into your automobile—sometimes alone, sometimes with one or more children or a spouse. Your car becomes your home until finally you have no money for gas and the authorities impound it. Without clean clothes, a shower, and a home address and phone number, a job interview is out of the question. Once on the streets, the cold weather, the fear for one's life, and the humiliation of begging take their toll. In major cities the din of traffic noise is so loud and constant that it soon creates disorientation. People start talking loudly to themselves above the noise around them. In most metropolitan cities there are no public restrooms, so they are forced to violate public health standards and their own dignity in following nature's call. Their days are deafening and defeating, and their nights on or under cardboard boxes are terrifying.

Back to Johnny: We made some calls to San Diego and found

that he did, in fact, have a shelter and meals at a church there, which allowed him to use their address to receive his Social Security check when he wasn't with us. (The irony of government aid to the homeless is that the individual must have a home address to receive their assistance check! While if they had a home, they likely would not need government assistance! Hundreds of thousands of dollars are returned to the government unopened.)

One of the proudest days in Johnny's life, and in the life of our congregation, was the morning he was publicly received into membership. He had been given a black suit, a white shirt, and a tie and had washed his hair and oiled his skin as he stood up there in front of his new family, tattered Bible in hand. There wasn't a dry eye in the house. The congregation had come to expect his often bizarre behavior of directing the choir (or at least the hymnals in front of him) while standing in his pew, preaching loudly along with me in a somewhat less coherent language with dramatic gestures, and greeting folks at the refreshment table after church, going home with them occasionally to use their showers. Some of our folks took him to the VA doctor and helped him fill out paperwork for public assistance, but tried unsuccessfully to find him employment. He was, as he told us, "overqualified." One week we didn't see him in church. Then another . . . and another. We found the church in San Diego which he used to call home, but they too had not seen him in months.

None of us knows what became of Johnny.

What we did discover is that we needed him even more than he needed us.

Poverty and homelessness are not partisan issues. They cut across all party lines. "Opportunity and poverty in this country cannot be explained by either the American Myth [of Horatio Alger] that hard work is a panacea for all ills, or by the Anti-Myth that the system imprisons the poor. Relief will come, if at all, in an amalgam that recognizes both the society's obligation through government and business, and the individual's obligation through labor and family—and the commitment of both [the] society and [the] individual through education."[25]

"Those who oppress the poor insult their Maker," the Bible says.[26] But the harder question is, how are the poor to be helped— By a handout or by a second chance? By charity or by justice? By voluntary contribution or by humanitarian legislation?

Giving charity will always be necessary. Charity binds wounds and buries bodies. But doing justice is also necessary. Justice is much more than punitive. True justice seeks to prevent the cause of the problem. The Bible is less concerned with alleviating the effects of injustice than in eliminating the causes of it. . . . Compassion and justice are companions, not choices. We can each be effective at the personal level as we do what we can to treat the symptoms of the many problems around us: social, economic, and spiritual. But we need to band together as a church, a temple, a mosque, a corporation, a community, a town, a country, and a common world to remedy the causes of . . .

the pain and the prejudice . . .
the hatred and horror . . .
the starvation and stockpiling . . .
the ignorance and illiteracy . . .
the inequality and injustice . . .
the disease the death . . .
plaguing all of us all over the world.

None of us has all the answers. But many of us are attempting to ask the right questions—and we have seen miracles happen. As fellow human beings living on the same planet, each of us has a heart that beats with the love of God for all people, whether of high or low estate. And each of us has the ability, and the responsibility, to do something, however small, to move our great country toward a more compassionate and just society for all people.

If religion ends with the individual, it ends. But together we can forge a new model for civilization. Together we can make straight those dirty, unsafe Jericho roads where children of God fall into ditches and die unnoticed. Together we can prepare the Way of the Lord in the wilderness of poverty and hopelessness.

It is not the poor who are the problem in America. It is the sin of poverty in the world's most prosperous, industrious, innovative, and generous nation. We can do better. We must do better. And when we do . . .

- that woman in the ditch at the side of the road will thank us,
- Johnny and his friends on the bus will thank us, and
- Jesus will smile down at us,

because we finally figured out what it means to be "born again."

CHAPTER 6

GANDHI'S SEVEN DEADLY SOCIAL SINS

"Without a vision, the people perish."
—PROVERBS 29:18

I want to begin with a couple of disclaimers: First, this chapter, "Gandhi's Seven Deadly Social Sins," is not about a finishing school's social graces . . . nor is about proper dining etiquette at the boss's house! Second, as far as we know, Mahatma Gandhi was not concerned with how one ate one's food. His concern was always that there was enough food for all to eat.

Gandhi was more concerned about the discrepancy between two realities: a common earth which can produce much more than the real needs of its human inhabitants . . . and a common misperception that there is not enough of anything to go around.

And I don't mean just food. I mean health, power, wealth, work, morality, conscience, character, humanity, goodness, and sacrifice. We presently have all that we might ever need of these graces. They are also in our families, our houses of worship, our schools, our businesses, our governments, our medical centers, and our entertainments.

Yet there is this ongoing misperception that we don't have enough of what we need.

Dr. Martin Luther King said it well: "Our lives begin to end the day we become silent about those things that matter. . . . The time is always right to do right."

That is why I choose to celebrate Dr. King's life and message with a profound declaration from another famous humanitarian, Mahatma Gandhi.

Gandhi, arguably India's Martin Luther King, was more concerned with our Social Sins than with our Personal Sins. It is not our private "spiritual" sins which kill us—sins like lust, gluttony, greed, sloth, wrath, envy, and pride. The greater damage to the common good of a society, according to Gandhi, is the way we make public decisions. A preoccupation with the personal to the preclusion of the social is bad religion. Good religion is not about making people fit into society better. Good religion is about asking whether a society is truly worth fitting into.

As Bill Coffin put it, "Truth is always in danger of being sacrificed on the altars of good taste and social stability. . . . We must guard against being too individualistic and elitist in our understanding of spirituality. Some Christians talk endlessly about the importance of one's interior life and how to develop it more fully, forgetting that Christ is born to bring hope and joy also to whole communities of people—the exiles, the deported, the tortured, and the silenced." [27]

Mahatma Gandhi predicted that seven things would destroy us:
> Politics without Principle,
> Wealth without Work,
> Commerce without Morality,
> Pleasure without Conscience,
> Education without Character,
> Science without Humanity, and
> Worship without Sacrifice.

All of these have to do with social, political, and economic conditions and community, not merely with private inner spirituality.

First is the Deadly Social Sin of Politics without Principle.

"The key to a healthy society," as Stephen Covey writes in his book, *Principle-Centered Leadership*, "is to get the social will, the value system, aligned with correct values. You then have the compass needle pointing to true north. . . . But if you get a sick social will behind the political will that is independent of principle, you could have a very sick organization or society with distorted values."[28]

"Humanity should come from faith, particularly when you link it to power."[29] That was Martin Luther King's logic. But what we are seeing today is so many fundamentalists around the world using their religions for power, but not for good.

The Second Deadly Social Sin is Wealth without Work.

Covey says, "This refers to the practice of getting something for nothing—manipulating markets and assets so you don't have to work or produce added value, just manipulate people and things. Today there are professions built around making wealth without working, making much money without paying taxes, benefiting from free government programs without carrying a fair share of the financial burdens, and enjoying all the perks of citizenship of country and membership of corporation without assuming any of the risk or responsibility."[30]

In what would be his final speech, Dr. King warned that "when machines and computers, profit motives and property rights, are considered more important than people, the giant triplets of racism, extreme materialism, and militarism are incapable of being conquered." Since that speech in 1967, the "glaring contrast of poverty and wealth" that King warned us about has grown abysmally wider. We would do well to re-think Gandhi's deadly sin of Wealth without Work in our world today.

The Third Deadly Social Sin is Commerce without Morality or, to say it another way, Business without Ethics.

"The most dangerous criminal," said King, "may be the man gifted with reason but with no morals."

In his book, *Moral Sentiment*, which preceded *Wealth of Nations*, the Scottish Presbyterian Adam Smith explained how foundational to the success of our system is the moral foundation: how we treat each other, the spirit of benevolence, of service, of contribution. "To Adam Smith, every business transaction is a moral challenge to see that both parties come out fairly. Fairness and benevolence in business are the underpinnings of the free enterprise system called capitalism. Our economic system comes out of a constitutional democracy in which minority rights are to be attended to as well. The spirit of the Golden Rule, or of 'win-win,' is a spirit of morality, of mutual benefit, of fairness for all concerned."[31]

One writer has suggested that "[a]s our unsustainable affluence and orgy of consumption continue to fuel economic and energy policies . . . and threaten the very existence of the planet, we might remember that King called for "a radical revolution of values" in the United States, a "shift from a thing-oriented society to a person-oriented society."[32]

The Fourth Deadly Social Sin is Pleasure without Conscience.

"The chief query of the immature, greedy, selfish," says Covey, "has always been: 'What's in it for me? Will this please me? Will it ease me?' Lately many people seem to want these pleasures without conscience or sense of responsibility, even abandoning or utterly neglecting spouses and children in the name of doing their thing. But independence is not the most mature state of being ? it's only a middle position on the way to interdependence, the most advanced and mature state. . . .

"Often on plane flights I'll scan the magazines directed at executives, noting the advertisements. Many of these ads, perhaps two-thirds of them, invite executives to indulge themselves without conscience because they 'deserve it' or have 'earned it' or 'want it,' and why not 'give in' and 'do what you've always wanted to do?' The seductive message is, 'You've arrived. You are now a law unto yourself. You don't need a conscience to govern you anymore.'"[33] The modern consensus is, "If I can do it, I should do it." The time has come for us to rethink that.

The Fifth Deadly Social Sin is Education without Character.

Human beings must "not be judged by the color of their skin, but by the content of their character," Dr. King demanded at his 1963 March on Washington.

"Purely intellectual development without commensurate internal character development makes as much sense as putting a high-powered sports car in the hands of a teenager who is high on drugs."[34] Yet that is what we do by not focusing on character, as well as academic development, in our schools and homes.

King's passion to democratize learning and abolish segregated schools for the upper elite was not based on an educational philosophy of "the lowest common denominator." It was based on a vision of "the highest achievement possible." Martin didn't look at that young black student walking into that white high school and say to himself, "Now we finally got it made! Just like the white folks! Now we can show 'em who's in charge!" Dr. King looked at that young student and must have thought to himself, "A mind is a terrible thing to waste. Today the world has another chance to survive."

The Sixth Deadly Social Sin is Science without Humanity.

"Science knows no country," King once preached, "because knowledge belongs to humanity." Michael Eric Dyson's important book, *I May Not Get There with You*, reminds us that toward the end of his life, King underwent a dramatic transformation from liberal reformer to radical who believed that "a reconstruction of the entire society" was necessary in the United States. I can imagine that if he had been allowed to live, which is quite unlikely, Martin Luther King would have pushed his drive for student literacy into the fields of global science and technology, each with a spiritual and humanitarian base. If science becomes all technique and technology, it quickly degenerates into a sin against humanity. "The earth is the Lord's and the fullness thereof." So let's see what it can teach us about ourselves.

The Final Deadly Social Sin is Worship without Sacrifice.

"Without sacrifice we may become active in a church but remain inactive in its gospel. In other words, we go for the social façade of religion and the piety of religious practices. There is no real walking with people, or going the second mile, or trying to deal with our social problems that may eventually undo our economic system. It takes sacrifice to serve the needs of other people—the sacrifice of our own pride and prejudice, among other things."[35]

Lamenting religious leaders who accommodated the war, King defended nonviolence on two fronts. "Have they forgotten that my ministry is in obedience to the one who loved his enemies so fully that he died for them?" he asked. "What then can I say to the Vietcong, or to Castro, or to Mao? Can I threaten them with death or must I not share with them my life?"

"We will stop communism by letting the world know that democracy is a better government than any other government," he told his congregation, "and by making justice a reality for all of

God's children." When discouragement invaded his own staff, he exhorted them to rise above fear and hatred alike. "We must not be intimidated by those who are laughing at nonviolence now," he told them on his last birthday.

"I say to you that our goal is freedom," he said in what, tragically, would be his final Sunday sermon. "And I believe we're going to get there because, however much she strays from it, the goal of America is freedom."

Only hours before his assassination, King startled an aide with a balmy aside from his unpopular movement to uplift the poor. "In our next campaign," he remarked quietly, "we have to institutionalize nonviolence and take it international." Then they killed him.

Someone once said that a politician is someone who thinks only about the next election, whereas a statesman or stateswoman thinks about coming generations. We have had too many politicians over the generations of this country who have played to the shady side of human nature.

In 1939 in his Address to the Nation, President Franklin Delano Roosevelt said, "My fellow Americans, progress is not measured by how much we add to the abundance of those who already have a great deal, but rather by how much we do for those who have too little." As Martin Luther King declared, "A nation which spends more money on military defense than on programs of social uplift is approaching spiritual death."

Those words need to be heard again today around the world. Friends, our time is running out. We need to raise up a generation of statespeople in this country, not just politicians. Statespeople who believe in patriotism, but who everyday question why it must end at our borders. The call is to women and men alike, like many of you reading this book, children of God...

> "Who more than life their country love,
> and mercy more than life!
> America! America! May God thy gold refine,
> 'Till all success be nobleness,
> and every gain divine!"

CHAPTER 7

GET OVER IT . . .
GET ON WITH IT!

Harry Truman opened the door to Eleanor Roosevelt's study. Mrs. Roosevelt had not wept. "Dry-eyed, she turned to face the Vice President. She placed her hand on his shoulder. 'Harry,' she said, 'the President is dead.' He blinked behind his glasses. It was as though he could not comprehend the words. . . . The county politician from Missouri had come to the ultimate glory. Everyone in the room had detected the possibility of Franklin Delano Roosevelt's death for a year; they had learned to live with it and to lie to each other hopefully.

"There was, they learned, a difference between the possibility and the stunning actuality. It was death and much more than death. The man lying on the bed under the Navy cape had been the power and the repository of individual leadership for a longer span of time than any other American. A world had expired at 3:35 p.m. in Georgia; the consummate politician, the main fuse, the idealist, the jolly father who spanked and rewarded had ceased to function, and all of the strength and might was now in the hands of the dapper man in the bow tie. . . .

"'Is there anything I can do for you?' Truman said to Mrs. Roosevelt. She smiled and looked down at the figured rug. 'Is there anything we can do for you?' she said. 'For you are the one in trouble now!'

"'Harry Hopkins cursed, and said '. . . now we've got to get to work on our own. This is where we've really got to begin. We've had it too easy all this time because we knew he was there and we had the privilege of being able to get to him. Whatever we thought was the matter with the world, whatever we felt ought to be done about it, we could take our ideas to him, and if he thought there was any merit in them, or if anything we said got him started on a train of thought of his own, then we'd see him go ahead and do it. And no matter how tremendous it might be or how idealistic, he wasn't scared of it. Well—he isn't there now, and we've got to find a way to do things by ourselves.'"

That's how Jim Bishop tells the story of F.D.R.'s last day.[36]

Life has a way of throwing us some pretty tough curve balls, doesn't it? We know what we want to accomplish in life . . . and how . . . we set goals for ourselves . . . we get our ducks in line . . . we establish bench marks . . . we awaken each day with a sense of purpose and direction. Then all of a sudden life careens out of control . . . stuff happens . . . and our future plans are blown to smithereens. Everything we have given our hearts to falls apart. Now what?

Jesus's disciples are standing together, committed to his program, raring to go, ready to follow him anywhere, and then *poof*, in the blink of an eye he is gone, *vanished*. They look up toward the heavens with disbelief. *"What just happened? He was right here talking to us, pumping us up. He made us believe that we could change the world. Now what?"*

Then they see the images of two figures in white speaking to them. *"Men of Galilee, why do you stand looking up toward heaven? He will appear to you. But not now. Do what you must do. Get over it . . . and Get on with it."*

How many of us have had someone in our life whom we thought would always be there for us, whom we counted on to make the world right for us—a parent, a teacher, a spouse, a lover, a friend, a companion, a colleague—only to find one day that they are gone—vanished. They stop calling . . . they're too busy . . . they have other plans . . . they have their own life . . . they lose their life. Whatever it is, they are no longer there for us.

What do you do when the bottom falls out of your life? Where do you find the power to go on, the reason to live, and the passion to begin again to make the world right?

Cory ten Boom, who lost both her parents in a German Death Camp, went through that horrible tragedy and came out stronger on the other side. "There is no pit so deep," she says, "that God is not deeper still. When we fall, we fall into the arms of God."

C.S. Lewis echoed that same faith: When we find ourselves unraveled, undone, we are actually standing on the precipice of a new adventure. "It occurs," he writes, "when the boy who has been enchanted in the nursery by stories from the Odyssey buckles down to really learning Greek. It occurs when lovers have gotten married and begin the real task of learning to live together. In every department of life it marks the transition from dreaming aspiration to laborious doing."[37]

When life throws us a curve ball, sometimes the greatest lesson we can learn is to embrace unpredictability. "Get over it . . .Get on with it."

According to Stephen Pressfield's book, *The War of Art*, "resistance" is the derailing force we experience when we attempt any potentially good thing—a painting, an article, a marathon or a marriage. It strikes anyone who hopes to move to a higher plane—in relationships, spirituality, academics, creative work, or business.

"If you were meant to cure cancer or write a symphony or crack cold fusion and you don't do it, you not only hurt yourself, even destroy yourself. You hurt your children, you hurt me, and you hurt the planet. You shame the angels who watch over you and you spite God Almighty, who created you and only you, with your unique gifts, for the sole purpose of nudging the human race one millimeter further along its path back to God."[38]

Some of us lost the living Christ when we lost our adolescence. We knew him personally as a child or a young adult—"He walked with us, and talked with us, and told us we were his own, and the joy we shared as we tarried there, none ever has ever known."—but as we look back, it seems that He was here for a while, but not anymore. He may come again some day—but in the meantime, he is not here. As Marcus Borg puts it, "Jesus had become for me a divine figure of the past, not a [human] figure of the present."[39]

Yet, Jesus' promise remains: "You will receive power when the Holy Spirit has come upon you, and you will be my witnesses . . . to the ends of the earth."

Knute Rockne, Notre Dame's football coach 80 years ago, is still one of the greatest coaches college football has ever known. "Rock," as he was known, wrote this prayer for his team:

"Dear Lord,
In the struggle that goes on through life
we ask for a field that is fair,
a chance that is equal with all the strife,
the courage to strive and to dare;
and if we should win, let it be by the code,
with our faith and our honor held high;
and if we should lose, let us stand by the road
and cheer as the winners go by."

That prayer needs to be lived out by each of us in our day.

"Where did he go?" we rightly ask. "How can I survive without her?" Yet if we choose to do so, we will see the ascended Christ there for us at those critical periods in our own lives when we have come to the end of our rope. When everything that has meant anything to us falls apart . . . when we fear that we will never again be loved, or needed, or able to accomplish our dreams . . . then we can 'look up,' see ourselves anew and afresh for the first time, and experience the God-given flow of life's essential energies bubbling up within us.

The same is true for families, communities, and nations. William Blake immortalized John Milton's unfulfilled vision for their beloved England, and he expressed it with passion:

"And did those feet in ancient time
Walk upon England's mountains green:
And was the holy Lamb of God
On England's pleasant pastures seen!

And did that Countenance Divine
Shine forth upon our clouded hills?
And was Jerusalem builded here
Among these dark Satanic Mills?

Bring me my Bow of burning gold:
Bring me my Arrows of desire:
Bring me my Spear: O clouds unfold!
Bring me my Chariot of fire.

I will not cease from Mental Fight,
Nor shall my Sword sleep in my hand:
'Till we have built Jerusalem
In England's green and pleasant Land."[40]

My friends, why do we stand looking up toward the heavens? Nothing happens there. Let's get over it . . . let's get on with it. This is where the action is, down here in the grit of daily life. Don't wait for Jesus to return in the clouds. He returns every time you and I take one courageous step for truth and justice, for hope and life and love in this place we call our earthly home.

As it was said of Jesus, Roosevelt, Martin Luther King, Jr., and so many others, so it needs to be said of each of us. "He isn't here now, and we've got to find a way to do things by ourselves." Because now he lives **within** us. Let us not "shame the angels who watch over us, and spite God Almighty, who created us for the sole purpose of nudging the human race one millimeter further along its path back to God."

Let each of us who would work to make the world a better place follow the pride and the passion of our exemplars who have gone before us. Let us *get over it*, and let us *get one with it*!

"Bring me my Bow of burning gold:
Bring me my arrows of desire:
Bring me my Spear: O clouds unfold!
Bring me my Chariot of fire.

We will not cease from Mental Fight . . .
'Till we have built Jerusalem
In America's green and pleasant land."

HOPE FOR
THE NATION'S
SOUL

"I believe that we are lost here in America, but I believe that we shall be found. . . . I think that the true discovery of America is before us. I think the true fulfillment of our spirit, of our people, of our might and immortal land, is yet to come. I think the true discovery of our own democracy is still before us."
—Thomas Wolf, from *You Can't Go Home Again*, (Perennial Classics, 1998, p. 741)

"For surely I know the plans I have for you, says the Lord, plans for your welfare and not for harm, to give you a future with hope."
—Jeremiah 29:11

CHAPTER 8

HOPE RISING
FROM THE ASHES

I t was a Thursday night just like any other Thursday night in any other city. Men and women had just arrived home from work. Children were playing or doing their homework. There was a certain tension in the air, but no one expected what was coming.

Suddenly, without warning, the entire city burst into flames. Children and parents were yelling and screaming, running for cover. The power lines went down, and the city blacked out. Telephones were dead, and sirens screamed through the streets. The only light was from the flames belching volcanically into the night.

Fire bombs gutted the Cathedral. Everything flammable was destroyed—the wooden roof, the heavy oak-beamed ceiling, the pews, the floor, and the great chancel screen. All that remained were the outer walls, the tower, and the spire. Never before had so much destruction occurred in so little time.

The city was Coventry, England. The night was Thursday, November 14, 1940. Coventry suffered the longest air raid of any one night on any British city during the Second World War.

The following morning, when firemen and townspeople rummaged through the smoldering remains on the floor of their once great Cathedral of Coventry, two signs of hope emerged: a charred cross of wooden beams and a rustic cross of nails. These two crosses stand today as dramatic symbols of hope rising from the ashes of destruction. Now, as then, they are powerful visual reminders, not only of the demonic violence human beings have unleashed on one another and the earth, but more importantly, of the divine possibilities of repentance, restoration and renewal—metaphors of the power of God to bring life out of death, order out of chaos, love out of hate, and a new social order out of social havoc.

A similar devastation took place some years ago in Los Angeles, California, not by the Germans but by fellow Americans. The cause was not the Second World War, but the public disbelief and outrage at the declaration of innocence following the trial of the police officers who beat Rodney King, Jr. All that good people had worked to accomplish over the past 25 years since the civil rights movement and the assassination of Dr. Martin Luther King, Jr. had gone up in smoke in a few short hours. The deplorable conditions of our city were tinder for this bombshell. Aerial photos of the city showed one of the largest cities in the nation burning out of control.

In fact, the fires began years before the Watts Riots and the brutal beating of Rodney King. Our country had been reeling from one staggering blow after another to the equality of all of our races, the dignity of every human being, and the right of every American to a decent education, an opportunity to work, a fair wage, an affordable shelter, basic health care, and adequate provision for their sunset years. These are necessities for every man, woman, and child in America.

Martin Fitzwater, then-President Bush's press secretary, was wrong. The blame for the Los Angeles riots was not the result of "failed" social welfare programs launched in the 1960's and '70's. The blame rests squarely on the shoulders of one administration after another that has refused to address the root problems in this country: the deep problems of economic injustice, latent racism, social isolationism, and moral and spiritual bankruptcy. Those are the problems. Not Medicare and Medicaid which give older Americans and the poor access to health care; not food stamps which help one in every ten Americans survive through the night; and not Head Start, which gives preschool kids a leg-up on self-development. Yes, welfare dependency is tragic. But worse is the apathy of those in power who refuse to provide satisfactory alternatives.

The problem that needs to be fixed is not the poor in our cities but the blind in our government and private sector. The problem is not the "unwashed multitudes" who live in filthy housing projects, but the filthy bankers who refuse to loan them money for business start-ups because of the color of their skin. The problem is not the voices of protest by young and old alike, those who are angry and unwilling to take it anymore. But rather, the problem is the silence of those in power to speak up for the rights of the underdog, the immigrant, and the dispossessed.

Riots are not strategies for change. Riots are rebellions against a lack of change. As the Reverend Jesse Jackson told those of us who walked Vermont Avenue in Los Angeles with him the day after the burnings and saw the charred and blackened ruins of those fires of anger and outrage which gutted entire buildings near our church: "Fire is the result of spontaneous combustion. When people are discarded, stockpiled into ghettos and barrios of desperation, they are like combustible material. It only takes a little spark to set them afire. It doesn't excuse the looting and the violence, but it says that the problems are so much deeper."[41]

Dr. Martin Luther King, Jr. said it 40 years ago: "Riots are the voices of the unheard." This is not mainly a race issue. Be very clear. It is a justice issue. Most poor people in this country are white. This is not an issue of laziness. Most poor people work every day that they can. They need more opportunity, not more indignity.

This is not mainly an issue of law and order. Yes, we need strong police and military to restrain violence and lawlessness, and to preserve law and order. Yes, we need to assure funding for adequate beat cops and hundreds of more police who will work together with community action groups. But NO, police are not the answer. No one needs police protection more than the poor, who suffer most from the ravages of crime. Violence flares up like wildfire when people have lost all hope for change and there appears to be no other option but to riot.

Bev and I were at the Central Post Office on 82nd and Vermont the day following the fires. It was the first day of the month. Those of you with limited income know the importance of the first and the 15th. That assistance check makes the difference between bread and milk and starvation; between paying your rent or living in your car—and then two weeks later when you've had to sell your car, living in a cardboard box. As hundreds of tense people stood quietly and orderly in line waiting to get into the post office for their life support checks, they were encircled by dozens of police and National Guard troopers who stood in readiness with their automatic weapons.

I was able to get through the line to ask the captain if I could be of any help as a clergyman to identify the few other clergy who were there, thinking we might form a line of peace and sanity between the people and the police in hopes of being a visible presence of peacefulness and nonviolence. He thanked me for offering, but assured me that all of those in line would be assisted before sundown, as in fact they were.

So I asked him for a couple gallons of the police's water and a box of cups. Then I walked the lines in the midday sun, offering a cup of cold water in the name of the unseen One to each of the folks who had been standing in the hot sun for hours and whose tempers were festering with the heat of the day. To a person, they were grateful and polite and glad to see a clergyperson there to help. I thought of Jesus' requests as he bore the cruel agony and weight of the cross up the Via de la Rosa. All that he asked for was a simple cup of cold water.

Sometimes what is needed is a cup of cold water to cool the angry flames of rage in the face of injustice. But sometimes what is needed is a flood of fiery passion for people in this country to wake up to our responsibility for our own—for federal, state, and county budgets to insure every person the basic needs of life. Sometimes what is needed is a river of living water bubbling up from inside the human heart, the inner spiritual life of which Jesus spoke as being the promise of God.

However, it is not simply one or the other—the physical or the social or the spiritual. I am outraged by the statement made by the pastor of one of our largest Los Angeles churches: "I'm grateful that Rodney King is alive," he said. "But my main concern is not that he gets his pound of flesh, but that he gets saved."[42]

A few days after the bombing of Coventry Cathedral, two signs of hope emerged from the ashes: The first was an 8-foot by 12-foot rugged wooded cross, formed out of two charred roof beams, tied together by wire and set in an old dust bin filled with anti-incendiary bomb sand. It was set at the east end of the ruined cathedral, over which some workman had written in large letters, "Father Forgive."

Some unknown Christian had spoken up against the violence and slaughter with the only voice he or she had. It is a sobering thought to stand in front of the cross today on the floor of Coventry Cathedral and envision the days when it was smoldering. It doesn't take much to imagine our Lord Jesus hanging on those charred beams, praying "Father, forgive them, for they know not what they do."

Oh, they knew very well what they were doing. Make no mistake. They knew, and still they did it. But what they did not know was the impact of their action upon the future and that through their killing of Love itself, the world would be saved, all because of that old wooden cross.

I thought about Scott Coleman, the 26-year-old young man who was attacked during the Los Angeles rebellions by people of a different color. He and his friend, Matthew Haines, were on their way to help two of their friends (one of whom was black) escape from the war zone. Matthew was killed by police fire, and Scott still has two bullets lodged in his arm. Even after his beating, despite his right to resentment and hatred, Scott said loud and clear, "I'm not going to hate them."

Christians in Coventry believed that. Their loved ones had been killed by Christians from Germany. But their first response was to get down on their knees and pray for their enemies. Praying does not excuse the abuses and the violence. But praying together somehow plants the seeds of hope. And working together waters them.

The second sign of renewal and hope found in the rubble of Coventry Cathedral was three large 14th Century hand-forged nails, which had been melded together by the heat of the flames into the shape of a cross. That "Cross of Nails" has becomes the symbol for an international Ministry of Reconciliation, one person helping another in the name of Christ for the cause of peace.

As soon as the war ended, Christians from Dresden, Germany, came to Coventry to rebuild its cathedral; and Christians from Coventry went to Dresden to rebuild its cathedrals. Today there is in Coventry Cathedral a Peace Shrine where 50 years ago there was only melted iron and charred beams.

Out of the fires of hell emerged the hope of the Kingdom of God. And it can happen again in our cities. As William Cullen Bryant put it, "Truth crushed to earth will rise again."

Historian Arnold Toynbee has said that some 26 civilizations have risen from the face of the earth. Almost all of them have descended into the junk heaps of destruction. The decline and fall of these great civilizations, he says, was not caused by external invasions, but by internal decay.

"If Western civilization does not respond constructively to the challenge to banish racism (and the 'underclass') in America, some future historian will have to say that a great civilization died because it lacked the soul and commitment to make justice a reality for all . . ."[43]

As Dr. King taught us, "The agony of the poor impoverishes the rich; the betterment of the poor enriches the rich. We are inevitably our brother's keeper, [our sister's sister]."[44]

The prophet Jeremiah, like Nehemiah, said it so clearly: "For I know the plans I have for you," says the Lord. "They are plans for good and not for evil, to give you a future and a hope."[45]

We all saw it on TV. In the midst of the flames and the violent riots, Rodney King stood there shaking, stammering, tears of grief in his eyes, and he pleaded for peace. He reminded us of a simple truth: "We can get along. We've got to. I mean, we're all stuck here for a while. Let's try to work it out."

The only alternatives open to us are nonviolent co-existence, or violent co-annihilation. We can kill each other with our words and our actions, or else we can lift each other up and out of the ashes. It's up to us.

God help us if we do not make the right choice.

CHAPTER 9

HOPE: THE FORCE THAT GIVES US MEANING

"Hope is a Waking Dream"
—ARISTOTLE

"Spring has now unwrapped the flowers;
Day is fast reviving.
Life in all her growing powers,
Toward the light is striving."
—(OXFORD BOOK OF CAROLS)

Hope is on the way! As the Bible says, "Faith is the substance of things hoped for, the evidence of things not seen."

Life is always striving toward the light. The frozen earth will not have the final word. The promise of the lush warmth and beauty of Springtime gives us hope. Hope for the abundance of nature . . . Hope for the blossoming of seeds long ago planted . . . Hope for a brighter future for all people . . . Hope for something new within ourselves . . . for a better nation, a better world, and a better earth.

Everything comes alive in the exuberance of Easter. We spring into a new way of being human. Where there was darkness, now there is light. Where there were problems, now there are possibilities. Where there were obstacles, now there are bridges. Where there was death, now there is life.

As Monsignor Oscar Romero—who was assassinated while at the altar during High Mass because of his pleading for the suffering and dying people of El Salvador—said a few days before he was killed: "If I am killed, I will rise up again in the Salvadorian people."

And so he did. He rose up again in the courage of those four American missionary women who died after their brutal torture . . . and again in the lives of hundreds of his peasant followers . . . with the same kind of Christian Hope and Faith which possessed those early disciples. Jesus rises up time and again in the courageous lives of good women, men, and children of all religions and none, in all nations, who stand for Hope against all the fear-filled rulers and ideologies of their day.

Christianity is more a call to rebellion than an insistence on narrow conformity . . . more a challenge than a set of certainties. As Marcus Borg and John Dominic Crossan chronicled Jesus' last days on earth in their book *The Last Week*: Jesus challenged the authorities with public acts and public debates. All this was his passion, what he was passionate about: God and the Kingdom of God, God and God's passion for justice. Jesus' passion got him killed."

Hope resists; whereas hopelessness adapts. Hopeful people criticize the present only because they hold a bright view of the future. They hate evil only because they so love the good. Wherever there is Hope, there is the Risen Jesus.

The great irony is that Hope and War have so much in common. Both are powerful, driving Forces of Life. War, like hope, is an enticing elixir. It gives us a purpose, a resolve, a cause. "Compared to war," General George Patton famously said, "all other forms of human endeavor shrink to insignificance. God, I do love it so."

That strong sense of meaning, of purpose . . . of calling . . . of nobility . . . of sacrifice . . . of communal struggle . . . was exactly what drove those early followers of Jesus after his resurrection. Except for them, it was not the Force of War which empowered them to accomplish great things . . . it was the Force of Hope.

"Hope begins in the dark; the stubborn hope that if you just show up and try to do the right thing, the dawn will come. You wait and watch and work: you don't give up." (Ann Lamont)

As Dr. Martin Luther King put it, "Our lives begin to end the day we become silent about things that matter."

War and Hope are each "Forces That Give Our Lives Meaning." But War cannot assure us of Hope. Only Hope can assure us of the end of War. And the gates of hell cannot prevail against that Hope. Hope is the power of the universe unleashed, in which...

. . . No suffering is too great to be comforted,

. . . No sorrow is too great to be consoled, and

. . . No structure of a selfish society is too great to be converted.

Easter Hope cannot be understood. It can only be experienced by stepping out in Faith and Hope. Only by taking such a risk will we encounter the real presence of Jesus who could not be consumed by death or corrupted by corruptible ministers, churches, theologies, or governments.

Our Hope should quell our fears, but never our courage. Compassion often demands confrontation. We have the audacity to proclaim, despite the evidence, that Hope has won. Easter Morning is the grand celebration of seemingly powerless love over loveless power. Easter reminds us that there is nothing stronger than Hope, not even death. Despair is not an option. Hope is the Force that gives us meaning.

CHAPTER 10

HOPE FOR ECONOMIC JUSTICE

"Poverty" is the word America hates to hear. To test this out, just mention the words "poverty" or "the poor" to anyone anywhere—especially at a party. Little you say after that will matter! People's attention disengages as soon as the word "poverty" is spoken. It's a word that puts people on the offensive. Poverty, shall we say, is "indelicate." It is a political liability. But in the richest and most powerful country in the world, it is also a reality.

According to a new study, one in eight Americans lives below the poverty line. That's one in eight too many. Over the last two decades, the United States has had the highest or near-highest poverty rates for children, individual adults, and families among 31 developed countries.[46]

When did economic injustice become yesterday's news? We long ago became bored with Katrina stories. Occasionally a photo in the paper or a TV news story grabs at our hearts. But not often enough. Even if we do get hooked with the obscenity of poverty, most of us feel we can't do anything about it.

Let me tell you Heather's story in her own words:

"As a young single mother of two I relied on welfare to get me through college. I remember sitting in a phone booth at Barnard College, pleading with the welfare specialist on the other end to give me my benefits. 'Sweetheart,' she told me, 'there's no way we're going to pay for you to go get more education than I have' . . .

"The truth is, it's miserable to be a poor mother in today's America," Heather says. "You're treated like a second-class citizen. Someone who breeds children in order to collect a fat welfare check. The reality couldn't be further from the truth. We are women who fight tooth and nail to provide decent lives for our children. It's a miracle that I survived my 5 years in the welfare system with my self-esteem intact. I remember clearly having people roll their eyes at me in the grocery line while I tore out my perforated food stamps. I remember waiting in huge waiting rooms for hours with two cranky children for an appointment with my benefits specialist. I remember waiting for sales on canned goods at my grocery store. I remember what it felt like to have one week until benefits and no more food.

"I have my Master's Degree now and my children are older. I no longer struggle like I used to. But I will always remember my humble roots and try to combat the stereotypes that are so ripe and prevalent about poor women. I will always fight for economic justice among the poor. It's our duty to help hold each other up. There's an ebb and flow to life. Sometimes we're the ones who need help, and sometimes we're the ones to give it."[47]

Heather's right. One in three Americans will experience a full year of extreme poverty at some point in their life. I think we need to talk about poverty and social justice. And I believe that our conversations should be filled with dignity, not shame. "A handout that serves as a salve for the conscience of the more fortunate is undignified. Blaming the poor for being poor is equally so. A system of welfare that traps families in poverty, which gives people something for nothing in return, robs them of their dignity. [And] a system of welfare that subsidizes industry and agriculture under the guise of economic health is undignified. . . . A stock portfolio and a Brooks Brothers suit does not make one dignified."[48]

Here in America, the wealthiest country in the world, there are 36 million people who are poor, 45 million without health insurance, and 25.5 million who are hungry. The average age of a homeless person is nine years old.

Theologian Bishop Krister Stendahl once quoted a rabbinic saying to the effect that theology is worrying about what God is worrying about when God gets up in the morning! "It would seem that God is worrying about the mending of creation, trying to straighten up the mess so that all of the groaning creation will be set free. To do this, God has to be worrying about those who have dropped through society's 'safety net,' about those who are victims of injustice and war, and about the destruction of their bodies, lives and environment."[49]

If you were a Jew in ancient Israel, you would have lived under the mandate, "There will be no poor among you" (Deuteronomy 15:4). "If your brother becomes poor, and cannot maintain himself with you, you shall maintain him" (Leviticus 25:35). Helping a poor person help himself was not an act of charity, it was an obligation of justice: "Do not withhold good from those to whom it is due, when it is in your power to do so" (Proverbs 3:27).

True to his Jewish religion and ethics, Jesus saw nothing inherently evil in money, wealth, or private ownership. While he regularly condemned materialism and the compulsive quest for wealth, Jesus never condemned wealth per se. Jesus saw nothing sinful in the ownership of houses, land, businesses, crops, clothes, and other economic goods. He had wealthy friends and followers (Luke 4:1); he stayed in the homes of wealthy people; he ate at their tables (Luke 11:37).

When a man in the crowd pled with Jesus to force his brother to share their father's inheritance him, Jesus replied, "Watch out! Your greed will kill you." Then he told him a parable of the demonic fear of death which forces us to amass fortunes, foolishly thinking that our wealth will keep us alive. Just as Lady Winchester (the widow of the inventor of the Winchester Rifle) found out, no amassing of wealth can keep us sane, nor can it keep us alive one second longer than our lifetime. If anything, our fearful grasping often shortens our life.

Jesus was not a socialist. He often spoke about wealth without condemning it (Matthew 13:44-46; 21:33-46). He did not criticize private ownership. He taught that children have an obligation to care for their parents (Matthew 15:3-9), and that his followers ought to be generous in their support of worthy causes (Matthew 6:2-4).

When he did call on people to renounce their possessions, it was often because people had made their possessions into a god (Luke 18:22-24). What Jesus condemned was not wealth, but the improper acquisition and use of wealth. Jesus did not pronounce God's judgment on wealth that resulted from honest labor, ethical management, careful stewardship, and wise investment. He did condemn wealth extracted from the poor by the scheming and dishonest.[50]

Like Isaiah before him, Jesus exhorted the people to "learn to do good; seek justice, rescue the oppressed, defend the orphan, and plead for the widow" (Isaiah 1:17). In other words, "love your neighbor as you do yourself."

"Those who oppose the poor insult their Maker," wrote the author of Proverbs 14:31. But the crucial question is: how are the poor to be helped—by charity or by justice, by voluntary contribution or by legislation?

"The primary problems of the planet arise not from the poor, for whom education is the answer; they arise from the well-educated, for whom self-interest is the problem."[51]

Justice is the moral code that guides a fair and equitable society. In Christian tradition, there are four ways God loves the world through us:

On the vertical axis there is Individual Charity (volunteering in a soup kitchen, for instance), and Individual Justice (standing up for the rights of others); on the horizontal axis there is Social Charity (contributing to programs which feed the poor, for instance), and Social Justice (changing the laws which keep poor people poor).

Social Charity addresses the effects of social sin; while Social Justice addresses the causes of such sins. Brazilian Catholic Archbishop Helder Camara famously said, "When I feed the poor, they call me a saint; when I ask why they are poor, they call me a communist."

The prophet did not say, "Let charity roll down like mighty waters," because giving without receiving is a downward motion. Amos said, "Let justice roll down like mighty waters, and righteousness like an ever-flowing stream." (Amos 5:24)

Social or Economic Justice is sometimes called "compassionate solidarity." The decision made by the First Presbyterian Church of New Canaan to buy only fair trade coffee might be considered an act of Social Charity. Social Justice would require the individual to act in an organized manner with others to hold social institutions accountable—whether government or private—to the common good. That is what Pope Paul VI called "the social conditions which allow people to reach their fulfillment more fully and more easily."

We have all seen those satellite photos of the planet. Looking at the earth from space, only a degree or two separates shadow from light. In the same way, comfort and misery are often just a few degrees apart. For most Americans, a chilled room can be bake-toasty with just a touch of a button—a few degrees are all it takes. At 98.6 degrees our bodies thrive, laugh, love—we live. A few degrees colder, hypothermia sets in, and we die. A few degrees warmer—fever overtakes us, and we die.

It is no less true of our political climate. Congress' cruel and reckless decision to cut billions of dollars from aid programs may seem like a small shift in a massive budget, but that tiny shift is critical to those who already live on life's margins. Budgets are moral documents. Our tax forms tell the truth about us.

If we say we care about the hungry but feast on corporate greed—if we say we love peace but kneel at the altar of an out-of-control war machine—if we say we cherish our children but steal their very futures through our own reckless spending—then all the excuses in the world cannot mask our true intentions. Economic growth is important, but it isn't everything.

Today, the future of our "little ones," whom Jesus so loved, is mortgaged by government debts that are increasing daily. . . . Every newborn American infant owes $20,000 in public debt when they draw their first breath. Public investment in education, health care, and housing is labeled "wasteful" and reduced or eliminated. So "the least of these"—children, the aged, the poor—are asked to bear the burden of controlling the public debt. This is an injustice. In is unfair, unchristian, and un-American.

My understanding of Jesus' love for all people, especially the young and the elderly, the poor and the disadvantaged, is a society in which no one is left behind, or left out, or deprived of dignity. As Franklin Roosevelt said in his Second Inaugural Address,

"The test of our progress is not whether we add to the abundance of those who have much; it is whether we provide enough for those who have too little."[52]

Life is more than money. Robert F. Kennedy once said: "The gross national product does not allow for the health of our children, the quality of their education, or the joy of their play. It does not include the beauty of our poetry or the strength of our marriages, the intelligence of our public debate, or the integrity of our public officials. It measures neither our wit nor our courage; neither our wisdom nor our learning; neither our compassion nor our devotion to our country; it measures everything, in short, except that which makes life worthwhile. And it tells us everything about America except why we are proud that we are Americans."

"Every gun that is fired," said President Dwight D. Eisenhower, "every warship launched, every rocket fired signifies, in the final sense, a theft from those who hunger and are not fed, those who are cold and are not clothed."

Many of my well-heeled friends are committed to helping the poor help themselves. Not only are they volunteering to tutor and feed God's children, but they are committed to Economic Justice Philanthropy. Not just "throwing money at a problem," but carefully investing in real solutions like creating jobs and developing self-reliance. Throughout the country Community Foundations are bringing tremendous entrepreneurial vision and business accountability to humanitarian development. I thank God for the commitment of so many of you in our churches to Social Philanthropy.

The way we treat our poor, our young, our elderly, and our underprivileged is the way we will be treated, says the Bible. "As you have done it unto the least of these," Jesus told us, "you have done it unto me."[53]

And whether we realize it or not, our investment in another human being does not diminish us . . . but makes us bigger . . . and better.

As James Forbes, the former Minister of Riverside Church in

New York City, put it, "Nobody gets to heaven without a 'Letter of Reference' from the poor!"

Thanks be to God.

CHAPTER 11

HOPE FOR
THE ENVIRONMENT

C arbon dioxide is heating up the Earth. Ice caps are melting, ocean levels are rising, hurricanes are intensifying, tropical diseases are spreading, and the threat of droughts, floods, and famines expands daily. Science Fiction? No. According to *Science Magazine*, the sea level could rise 20 to 55 inches by the year 2100, and it is likely that Bev's and my two granddaughters will be alive to see it.

An internal draft of The United States Climate Report, prepared for the United Nations and released in 2008 (more than a year overdue) by the Bush administration, cited growing risks to water supplies, coasts, and ecosystems around the U.S. from the anticipated temperature and precipitation changes driven by the atmospheric buildup of carbon dioxide and other heat-trapping greenhouse gasses.[54]

And it was just disclosed that by 2020 the U.S. will emit not less, but almost 20% more, gases that lead to global warming than it did seven years ago. The biggest source of these gases is the burning of fossil fuels, chiefly oil, coal, and natural gas. "We are on a path to exceeding levels of global warming that will cause catastrophic consequences, not just reducing the growth rate as the president is doing," says Chief Scientist Michael MacCracken, at the nonpartisan Climate Institute in Washington.[55]

These changes are more than an environmental issue, says Sir John Houghton, one of the world's leading climatologists; they represent a clear justice issue. The poorest people of the world will pay the greatest price for the effects of climate change. When the temperature increases by two degrees the sea will rise one meter (a little over three feet), and will displace 10 million people in Bangladesh alone. A rise of just two degrees more will cause extreme drought which could swallow Bangladesh and create 150 million refugees—again, among the world's poorest inhabitants.[56]

In a grim and powerful assessment of the future of the planet, the leading international network of climate scientists from more than 100 countries concluded for the first time in 2007 that global warming is "unequivocal" and that human activity is the main driver. The U.S., with about 5% of the world's population, is the largest polluter in the world, emitting a quarter of all greenhouse gases. The rest of the world, says Houghton, is looking to the U.S. to take the lead.[57]

Our passive tolerance of this clear and present danger to the earth is unconscionable and unacceptable. What in the Name of God are we doing to God's Creation? "The earth is the Lord's," said the Psalmist, "and all that is in it. The heavens are telling the glory of God; and the firmament proclaims his handiwork."[58]

But "the firmament today also proclaims some nefarious human handiwork—smog, acid rain, and an immense hole in the ozone layer . . . the average American car driven the average American distance—10,000 miles a year—releases annually into the atmosphere its own weight in carbon. . . . In Sweden all bodies of water are now acidic . . . while one Tennessee's-worth of the Amazonian rain forest is slashed and burned each year. As apparently there are more different species of birds in each square mile of that rain forest than exist in all of North America, we are silencing songs we have never even heard . . .

"No longer are our actions inhibited by wonder . . . We view nature essentially as a toolbox. Nature may have beauty but no purpose. It is there solely to serve human purposes . . . What we need beyond caution is reverence. What we need beyond practical fears are moral qualms. Unless nature is 'resanctified,' we will never see nature as worthy of ethical considerations similar to those that presently govern human relations."[59]

"Whatever befalls the earth befalls the sons of earth," said Chief Seattle 150 years ago. "Man did not weave the web of life; he is merely a strand in it. Whatever he does to the web, he does to himself . . . Continue to contaminate your bed and you will one night suffocate in your own waste."

I have titled these chapters "HOPE for... the Environment... Economic Justice... Terrorism... Nuclear Weapons... and Hope." But I am fully aware that 2,000 years ago Jesus had not even heard of global warming and nuclear weapons. However, his teachings and his lifestyle were in direct opposition to all attempts in every age to exploit the weak, the poor, human life, and nature itself.

Jesus' message is the same for every age. Life is sacred and anything which threatens life on our planet is anti-God. Faithful stewardship does not allow us to disregard and disrespect the world and its creatures, nor to wait for some glorious day in the future when all that is broken will be repaired and all that is evil will be made good. The time for that hard work is right now, by us, with God's help, before it is too late.

Jesus said, "From everyone to whom much has been given, much will be required; and from the one to whom much has been entrusted, even more will be demanded."[60]

Jesus wants the earth to live, not to die. When he wanted to encourage us in our futures, he pointed to the seeds being planted in good soil. When he wanted to help us in our anxiety, he pointed to the lilies of the field. When he wanted to reassure us about how much God cared for us, he reminded us how much God loved the sparrow. When he wanted to help us see how tenderly God loved us, he called forth the image of the mother and her chicks.

"And when he wanted and needed to speak with God in the most intimate way, it was to the great treasures of earth's beauty that Jesus turned—to the mountains, the wilderness, the sea, and the garden."[61]

We are not only stewards of God's earth, we are partners in creation. We are part of the earth and we live, eat, and breathe within what the Greeks called the *oikeumene*, "the house" of God's creation. Further, we are priests, mediators between God and the earth. Our role is to intercede for the Community of Life and speak and act on its behalf.

Pillaging of the earth, its resources, and its creatures is a colossal failure of responsible stewardship and a failure to honor God, to whom the earth belongs. As faithful stewards, we are obliged to do what we can individually and to call for public policies that preserve the natural riches of our nation and our world for the public good. To dismantle environmental laws and programs, measures that seek to protect creation and make it safer for our children, is immoral and a violation of our Christian duty.

I cannot say this strongly enough: Our planet is at risk, and in an order of magnitude never previously even imagined. There is no such thing as a Republican or Democrat, a liberal or conservative, a religious or a secular environment. We all breathe the same air and drink the same water. No longer is the survival unit a single nation nor a single anything; it is the entire human race plus the environment. As for Christians, it is time we stopped retreating from the giant social issues of the day into the pygmy world of private piety. The chief question is not, "What must I do to be saved?" but rather, "What must we all do to save God's creation?"

How does one person help save the earth? "Think Globally—Act Locally." There are specific things which you and I can do in our homes and businesses to turn this catastrophe around before it's too late.

Did you know that recycling one aluminum beverage can saves enough energy to run a 100-watt light bulb for 20 hours . . . that one recycled glass bottle saves enough energy to power the same bulb for 4 hours . . . and that one fluorescent bulb lasts 10 times longer than an incandescent one . . . that one recycled ton of paper saves 17 trees, 2 barrels of oil, 7,000 gallons of water, and 4,100 kilowatt hours of electricity—enough energy to power the average American home for 5 months . . . and that if everyone in the U.S. recycled just 1/10th of their newsprint, we would save the estimated equivalent of about 25 million trees a year?

You and I can do that. Some of us are already trying. But more than that must be done. The temperature rise this past decade has been enough to start melting every frozen thing on earth. The thawing tundra is releasing huge quantities of methane. Coral reefs may soon be gone. Scariest of all, the great ice sheets above Greenland and the West Antarctic appear to be melting faster than predicted. There is a very real chance of catastrophic rise in sea level, one that would endanger the world's coastal cities, inundate much prime farmland, and drive hundreds of millions of people from their homes—more refugees than we managed to create with all the bloody wars of the century we've just come through.[62]

We need a movement to combat climate change, and we need it fast. We need—at the very least—a federal commitment to cut carbon emissions 80% by 2050. And each of us can leverage our influence—with our personal priorities, our political power, and our financial investments.

Jeff Immelt, one of my congregants, promoted coal gasification at GE as a step toward curbing emissions of carbon dioxide from plants using coal. Coal-gasification plants emit less air pollution, use less water and leave behind less solid waster than convention- al coal-burning plants. GE joined with Lehman Brothers Holdings and some of the biggest U. S. power producers to urge the federal government to establish a national cap on global warming pollu- tion and take a leading role in global talks on combating climate change. That's fabulous! And that's just one man influencing one company![63]

I loved Bill Coffin's proposal that beyond saluting their flags and pledging allegiance to their country, our school children should pledge allegiance "to the earth, and to the flora, fauna, and human life that it supports; one planet indivisible, with clean air, soil, water, economic justice, freedom, and peace for all."

"To save the environment we need an Earth Covenant, a form of Magna Carta for the earth. Such a charter would expand the Universal Declaration of Human Rights so that some of the ethical considerations that presently govern human relations will be extended to nature as well. In religious terms, we need to recon- nect nature with nature's God. With Native Americans, we need to recognize our spiritual tie with every leaf and creature . . . to see ourselves not only as stewards but as 'priests of creation.'"[64]

How do you and I want to be remembered? As spoilers and exploiters? Or as redeemers and creators? Our calling—the calling of every human being—is to live a life worth the re-telling of it. When our children's children retell the lives of their grandparents, what will they say of us?

CHAPTER 12

HOPE FOR THE END OF NUCLEAR WEAPONS

The British call it busking. Busking is the art of Street Theater, doing live performances in public places. Benjamin Franklin was a busker of sorts. He composed songs, poetry, and prose about the evils of a current political situation, and then went out in public and performed them for the passers-by. When his father forbid him to continue busking, Franklin put his passion into promoting free speech.

"Nonviolent challenges to state power are an honored tradition in our history, and so is there repression, as far back as the trial and conviction of Socrates on trumped-up charges of blaspheming the gods and corrupting the youth of Athens. . . . To shine light on injustice usually means exposing and embarrassing those who perpetuate it. And that can be a dangerous thing."[65] That's why acts of civil disobedience are often acts of courage.

In order to show the precariousness of rank and power, Dionysius I held a banquet and had a sword suspended above the head of Damocles by a single hair . . . reminding his court of the ever-present peril of death.

Four hundred years after Dionysius, Jesus performed his own Street Theater in Jerusalem on what would become Palm Sunday. While the Roman governor, Pilate, entered the city from the West on a war horse in a grand procession of military power, Jesus, the "People's King," entered the city from the East on a borrowed donkey with a rag-tag band of followers. Jesus knew the prediction of the prophet Zechariah hundreds of years earlier—that a King of Peace would enter Jerusalem on a donkey to banish forever the war horse and the battle bow from the land.[66] Jesus knew that he was in that tradition, and therefore on a collision course with the Roman Empire. The sword of Damocles suspended itself above his head by a single hair.

While the fate of humanity hung in the balance.

"The only thing necessary for evil to triumph is for good men and women to do nothing." Which procession would you have joined that day? Caesar's . . . the Super Power of the day? Or Jesus' . . . the Peasants' Messiah?

Today the struggle continues between these competing allegiances. And once again the choice is clear: The Reign of Fear, Terror, and Nuclear Destruction; or The Reign of Peace, Partnership, and Mutual Salvation?

The closest the world has come to the brink of nuclear war was the Cuban Missile Crisis of October, 1962. The Soviets had installed nuclear missiles in Cuba, just 90 miles off the coast of the United States. U.S. forces were at their highest state of readiness. The fate of millions literally hinged upon the ability of two men, President John F. Kennedy and Premier Nikita Khrushchev, to reach a compromise. Over those 14 days the Sword of Damocles hung over the world by a single hair.

America was hysterical. In school we were taught that if the bomb dropped, we were to crouch down underneath our desks and cover our eyes. Many of you may remember that. Paranoia reigned. Many residents of New England built bomb shelters in their homes; "fallout shelters" we called them. During my pastorate at the First Presbyterian Church of New Canaan, my wife and I lived in the church's manse. Our home had a bomb shelter in the basement—a 10' by 10' concrete block domicile with two bunk beds, shelves for several weeks' supply of non-perishable foods, and a collapsible table—with a 1/4-inch wooden door to keep out the radiation!

Dr. David Brown tells me that one New Canaanite actually bought a railroad box car, dug a hole, and buried it his back yard as a bomb shelter! America was scared to death. Families were forced to verbalize the unspeakable question: Who would live and who would die?

Some years later, in late 1981, a local group of New Canaan citizens met to share their concerns and ideas about the prospect of worldwide unbridled nuclear proliferation. They came from business, law, medicine, churches, school, the arts, and public service and were part of what James Restor of The New York Times called "the rumblings of distant thunder before the storm."

Calling themselves "Nuclear Control and Reduction Now," they organized a Sunday Rally in the Common Room of the First Presbyterian Church. Leading them was the former Secretary of the Army, Stanley Resor (whose personal support to me in writing this chapter was invaluable), and our founding pastor, T. Guthrie Speers, along with former U.S. Ambassador William Attwood. Stan and Guthrie became the co-chairs of the group, with the support of Hud Stoddard, Jane Stoddard Williams, Anita Houston, Susan Hanson, Francis Salant, Chet Hansen, Jim Rogers, and many others. The primary purpose of this organization (which was renamed "The New Canaan Coalition for Nuclear Arms Control") was "to promote a world-wide arms freeze, with control and reduction now."[67]

That effort lasted 10 years through the end of the Cold War. And it was effective. Yet today the challenge is a thousand times greater.

As recently as 2005, former U.S. Secretary of Defense Robert McNamara called on religious groups to lead the push for global nuclear disarmament. "The U.S. no longer needs its arsenal of thousands of nuclear weapons," he said. "It's immoral, it's illegal, it's militarily unnecessary, and it's very, very dangerous in terms of accidental usage. . . . I can't think of anything more demanding of Christians than to rid the human race of this risk that, as Catholics say, is the danger of extinction."[68]

"If they do these things in the green wood," Jesus said, "what will they do in the dry?"[69]

Deadly depleted uranium has a half-life of over 4 billion years. Thousands of nuclear weapons are on hair-trigger alert. Nuclear war could start from a mad official decision, or a nuclear accident, or a minor technical failure.

The Doomsday Clock is again at five minutes to midnight. The unthinkable has become thinkable . . . the impossible possible . . . the worst scenario the first scenario. If 2,000 years ago we executed the Lord of Life in the green wood, what will we do in the dry?

In his play, *Caesar and Cleopatra*, George Bernard Shaw touched the raw nerve: "And so to the end of history, murder shall breed murder, always in the name of right and honor and peace, until at last the gods tire of blood and create a race that can understand."

The new international Badge of Courage, the new honorary degree of National Prestige, is now membership in the "Nuclear Club," the Club of Slaughter. How horrific!

"Nuclear weapons cannot become the Viagra of the national security state."[70]

"How can we Americans claim to be a responsible power when we profess humane ideals and threaten unlimited slaughter?"[71] "Nuclear superiority" is an oxymoron. I think it is pointless for any nation to try to be #1 in a nuclear contest. Madmen are not rational. They are impetuous. For them 'the first kill' is their reward, regardless of the consequences.

Worse still is the coupling of religion with war. As Pascal said, "people never do evil so cheerfully as when they do it from religious conviction." Nuclear Terror is non-denominational. The world will not be saved by a "Christian Bomb" nor an "Islamic Bomb," nor a "Jewish Bomb."

Shortly after the development of the nuclear bomb, theologian Reinhold Niebuhr concluded that "if these weapons were ever used against us, it would mean our physical annihilation; but if we ever used them against an enemy, it would mean our moral annihilation."[72]

You might think I am pessimistic about all of this. Far from it. For one thing, I trust in God, not in the 6:00 News! But more to the point, I once read a fabulous piece in *The Wall Street Journal* entitled, "A Call For A World Free of Nuclear Weapons" written by no less military statesmen than former Secretary of State, George Shultz, former Secretary of Defense William Perry, former Secretary of State Henry Kissinger, and former Chairman of the Senate Armed Service Committee, Sam Nunn. These Republicans and Democrats and other American leaders have declared that, since the Cold War, "reliance on nuclear weapons for [deterrence] is becoming increasingly hazardous and decreasingly effective." Deterring terrorist groups has become nearly impossible, and the peacekeeping value of nuclear weapons is more and more outweighed by the risk of their possible use.

Here is Sam Nunn, a man who was known as the leading Democratic hawk in the Senate, saying we have got to recapture this vision of eliminating nuclear weapons. Not just reducing nuclear dangers but eliminating these weapons. "We are at a tipping point," he says, "and we are headed in the wrong direction." We must work with leaders of the countries in possession of nuclear weapons to turn the goal of a world without nuclear weapons into a joint enterprise."[73]

Nunn acknowledges the danger of nuclear cheating and admits that any realistic disarmament plan would have to allow the U.S. to quickly reconstitute weapons if a threat emerged. But he has come to believe the greater danger is continuing on our current path. "I think we have to turn it around . . . You literally can't get there"—to a safer world, that is—"from here." "Twenty years ago *The Wall Street Journal* article "would not have been possible," he says. "I would not have been in that mood at that stage, and I said so." . . . "You can probably only get the achievement with the next generation," he predicts. "Probably none of the people who signed that [article] will be able to see it through. But the world has to see that direction. Perhaps then a younger generation will see that the goal is achievable."[74]

From President Eisenhower through President Bush, every one of our presidents of the United States has worked to stop nuclear proliferation and decrease weapons of mass destruction. Now is the time, declares the Journal's article, to begin to eliminate them completely.

Pilate's grand procession from the West that first Palm Sunday embodied all the power, glory, and violence of the empire that ruled the world. Jesus' simple procession from the East embodied an alternative reality: the Kingdom of God's justice and peace. This "Clash of Empires"—between the Kingdom of Caesar and the Kingdom of God—is being played out again in our world today. In one sense, we lost the first round. We cannot afford to lose the next.

The central theological question facing humanity today is

whether we will continue to be held captive by the claim of "nuclear demonology," that in death lies our hope for life.

When President Carter and Premier Brezhnev met in a formal ceremony to sign the Salt II Nuclear Arms Treaty, the leader of the world's foremost atheistic nation placed his hand on Mr. Carter's shoulder and said: "If we do not succeed, God will not forgive us."[75] That gesture could be interpreted cynically as mere manipulation and deceit. Or it could be interpreted faithfully as the only hope for a world gone mad.

We have a choice during Holy Week. We can turn away, wash our hands as Pilate did, cower in our private cocoons of personal fulfillment and public irresponsibility, and pretend that Damocles' Sword is not swinging above us by a single hair. Or we can do what Jesus sought to do: stop forever the hands of the Doomsday Clock at five minutes to midnight. "The choice goes on forever 'tween the darkness and the light."[76]

May God give us courage for the living of these days.

CHAPTER 13

HOPE FOR THE END
OF TERRORISM

B efore boarding the plane on that bright, clear September morning the young man telephoned his wife to tell her, three times, that he loved her. Only the night before, he had written her a love letter. It began, "My love, my life. My beloved lady, my heart . . .I love you and will always love you." It ended, "I am your prince and I will pick you up. See you again!! Your man always."

Unlike the other passengers who said good-bye to their family members that morning, however, the 26-year-old Lebanese student, Ziad Jarrah, knew that he would not be seeing them again. He boarded United Airlines Flight 93 on the morning of September 11, 2001, with no intention of ever stepping off the plane.[77]

Several months ago senior al-Qaeda figure Khalid Sheikh Mohammed confessed to the world that he was the "principal architect" of that day of horror.

If there is one thing the world has learned since the terror and destruction of that fateful day it is that "terrorists are neither crazy nor amoral. They come from all parts of the world. They come from many walks of life. They fight for a range of different causes. Some have support from the communities from which they come; some do not. . . . They come from all religious traditions and from none. One thing they do have in common: they are weaker than those they oppose."[78]

In September 2001 the human race did not suddenly produce a new breed of evildoers. The forces driving terrorists today are similar to the forces that have driven revolutionaries in other countries and in other times throughout history. What has changed is their ability to inflict such horrendous death and destruction.

Louise Richardson, in her stunning new book, *What Terrorists Want*, tells of an ancient trilogy of terrorism and religion. There were the Zealots (also called the Sicarii) from Biblical times, the Assassins from the medieval period, and the Thugi (or 'Thugs'), up to the modern times.[79]

The goal of the first group, the Jewish Zealots of Jesus' day, was to eliminate Roman rule in Palestine. They sought to inspire a mass uprising against the Roman Empire and believed that the spiral of violence would herald the arrival of the Messiah. Their religious fanaticism was unbridled. Every concession from the Romans was met with another atrocity by the Zealots. Their objective was the same as terrorists today, to create massive public panic, fear, and terror. Their weapon was the Sicarii, a dagger, which they would pull from beneath their clothes, stab their victim, and then disappear into the crowd.

At least two of Jesus' twelve disciples had been Zealots. One was named "Simon Zealot." But the other disciple whom I think might well have been swayed by the Zealot cause was Judas. It was Judas, remember, who "turned Jesus over" to the Chief Priests and the temple police with a kiss. I do not believe he did it for the money. I think he intentionally tried to provoke Jesus and the other disciples to go public, to take up arms against the Romans and their sympathizers, believing that Jesus would be forced to violence and declare himself to be the long-awaited political and military King of the Gentiles and Savior of the Jews.

There was an early Jewish tradition of a "Divine War of Extermination," called "the ban," or *herem*, which required the killing every human being and animal in every town that would not convert to the God of the Jews—to completely annihilate them. The Book of Joshua mentions 31 kings defeated in bloody battles and after every battle the city and everyone in it was slain by the sword, as ordered by the Lord. (Joshua 12:24)

Jesus, however, refused to take up the sword. He turned their weak violence into powerful nonviolence. "No more of this!" he said. And he touched the Roman soldier's ear and healed him. In that symbolic act, Jesus turned the "military industrial complex" upside down. "My kingdom," he told them, "is not like this one. Choose this day whose kingdom you will serve."

The second group of religiously-motivated fanatics were the Islamic Assassins, who operated in the latter part of the Middle Ages, from the 11th to the 13th Centuries. The Assassins were a fanatical and murderous Shia Muslim sect. They were inspired by

the goal of purifying Islam through jihad, or "holy war." As with
the Zealots, their strategy was a policy of public assassination by
stabbing, and their victims were orthodox religious leaders who
refused to hear their warnings. They created their own state out of
mountain fortresses, where they welcomed refugees. They trained
recruits, developed their organization of complex sympathetic
cells in urban centers, and dispatched their members to carry out
assassinations. They would send a young recruit into the house
of an intended victim to develop a personal relationship before stabbing him in front of his family. Unlike the Zealots who
quickly disappeared into the crowd, the Assassin considered it
shameful to escape, and would wait for the ultimate glorification
of being beaten to death or arrested and executed as a martyr.

The third wave of religious terrorists was the Hindu Thugi, who
operated in India for about 600 years before being annihilated by
the British in the 19th Century. They believed that their goddess
Kali killed an enormous monster that devoured humans as soon as
they were created. But for every drop of blood another monster
emerged. Since Kali represented the energy of the universe, the
Thugi believed that they were obliged to supply her with the blood
necessary to keep the universe in equilibrium. The Thugs, as they
were called, were the first precursors of state-sponsored terrorism.

All three of these terrorist movements were deeply religious, as
have been countless Christian sects over the years who were convinced that violence was the ultimate answer to religious persecution. This observation raises the question: "How does religion
become evil—whether it be Jewish, Christian, Muslim, Hindu, or
whatever? What are the warning signs of corruption in religion?"

First, there is the delusion of Absolute Truth claims, which is
present in each of our religions. If we see ourselves as having the
truth and other people as living in error, it is a short step to . . . the
second delusion of Blind Obedience. Our inability to see religious
and scriptural language as metaphorical can create terrible consequences. That is why it was possible for centuries for Christians to
support the institution of slavery with their Biblical texts. That is

why young Palestinian suicide bombers are video-taped reciting Koran promises of paradise . . .

Third is the national commitment to a Theocracy, a political/religious/military society in which a nation's riches and warfare are believed to be the blessing of God's favor . . .

This is inevitably followed by the conviction that the end justifies the means, which ultimately results in the declaration and unbridled religious passion of a Holy War.[80]

People who live without hope, which is the majority of people on our planet, live in depression. Depression, when internalized deeply enough, can lead to murder and mayhem. Terrorism has combined the two within a religious framework of Divine Blessing and Rewards. "Terrorists see the world in Manichean, black-and-white terms. . . . They have a highly oversimplified view of the world in which good is pitted against evil and in which their adversaries are to blame for all their woes. They tend to act not out of a desire for personal gratification but on behalf of a [repressed] group with which they identify."[81]

The urge to declare war in response to an atrocity on the scale of September 11 is very powerful, and the decision to do so is very understandable. But many of us believe it is also very unwise. One does not fight fire with fire. You can't win a war against terrorism; you can only exacerbate it. What we need is an alternative strategy, a strategy that replaces the very ambitious goal "to rid the world of the evildoers" and "to root terrorism out of the world" with a more modest and more achievable goal of containing the threat from terrorism.[82]

The greatest challenge ahead of us is that "Terrorism will have to be confronted in a world in which controlling belief systems differ radically, not only between different cultures . . . but even between different moral perspectives within any one tradition. Terrorism will not be stamped out by the mere escalation of resolve, however vehement or single-minded. . . . To be faithful in the face of terrorism does not consist of having a strategic blueprint for particular actions.

The danger terrorism poses may be less in what it can do to harm us than in what it prompts us to do to harm ourselves. If we lose confidence in our own best inclinations, thinking that threats can only be dealt with by mounting counter threats, that deceit can only be met by clandestine cleverness, surprise only offset by counter surprise, and violence stemmed only by counter violence, terrorism will have reshaped us even if think we have overcome it.

If we curtail freedoms in the process of defending freedom, what is the benefit? We need a positive resurgence of our noble convictions rather than the embrace of strategies that merely mirror the stances of those we seek to oppose. Such a response to terrorism is possible only in the context of a vital practice of a faith deeply rooted in compassion.[83]

Terrorism is a sign of despair. "Suicide bombers announce that theirs is a meaningless life. Their religious mentors play on their despair by suggesting that the cause of their hopelessness is the spiritually decadent West. 'Allah's martyrs' are then promised a glorious reward if they die while spreading pain and fear among their enemies. That kind of belief will never be deterred by American might.

"When Vice President Cheney set the nation's policy by saying that we must 'destroy them before they strike us,' it seems to me that we simply do not understand the nature of terrorism. Nothing can protect this nation from those who are willing to sacrifice their own lives in the attempt to strike out at the enemy. Our military forces are victorious in the conventional kind of retaliatory war, but in the process of that victory they create more despair in the defeated nations and thus more terrorists....

"When will we understand that the causes of terrorism are not only hatred and retribution, but also poverty, hopelessness, despair and the lack of education and opportunity, all enflamed by religious vindication? Terrorism is the response of the powerless to their powerlessness. When we attack the symptoms, all we do is to suppress the problems. . . . Instead of making our world safer, are we not just creating the breeding places for more and more terrorists?

"One tenth of the money we have poured into the wars in Afghanistan and Iraq, to say nothing of the money we now spend on national security, could fund effective programs aimed at education, opportunity, dignity, hope and freedom among the despairing masses of Muslim young adults. In the words of the peace movement, created by the Vietnam War: 'When will we ever learn? When will we ever learn?'"[84]

Throughout his life, Jesus modeled the best use of power. In one Gospel story after another, we see him using his power to heal, to instill life, to feed others, to offer hope, and to hold leaders accountable. "When he saw the crowds, he had compassion for them, because they were harassed and helpless, like sheep without a shepherd."[85] That's how he won their allegiance, by moral strength, not by force.

With his constant care for the poor, the outcasts, and the powerless, Jesus demonstrated his understanding that poverty, too, is a weapon of mass destruction. He taught his followers that they were not to return violence when it was directed at them (Matthew 5:38-48; Luke 6:27-36). That did not mean that he expected them to be passive victims, but rather that through endurance and their willingness to sacrifice that they could outlast and overcome evil (Matthew 24: 9-14; Luke 21:9-19). . . . And finally, in the darkest and most frightening times, Jesus said to his followers, "Be not afraid . . . " (Matthew 28:10). . . .

We, too, must follow Jesus' example and reject the false prophets of our day. We must "be not afraid" as we strive to use our nation's power and authority in the world to find new solutions that serve the people, protect the innocent, and preserve the good while seeking "justice for all."

The tragedy is that the massacre of 9/11 was a lost opportunity. It could have been a revolutionary moment to help Americans deepen the quality of our suffering by identifying with masses of others around the world who suffer, and to help us abandon the American illusion of invincibility.

We could have said to the world, "We will respond, but not in kind. We will not seek to avenge the death of innocent Americans by the death of innocent victims elsewhere, lest we become what we abhor. We refuse to ratchet-up the cycle of violence that brings only ever more death, destruction and deprivation. What we will do is build coalitions with other nations. [Not only will we shore up our security], but we will share intelligence, freeze assets and engage in forceful extraditions of terrorists. [We will] do all in [our] power to see justice done, but by the force of law only, never by the law of force."[86]

That is the commitment of a great nation.

Abraham Lincoln, who certainly knew that some wars must be fought, still observed, "Am I not destroying my enemies when I make friends of them?"

"When will we ever learn? When will we ever learn?"

CHAPTER 14

TO SEEK A NEWER WORLD...

"We ourselves feel that what we are doing
is just a drop in the ocean.
But that ocean would be less
because of that missing drop."
— MOTHER THERESA

After the sneak attack, crowds gathered outside the White House and sang "God Bless America." Soldiers armed with machine guns guarded government buildings. The FBI began rounding up suspicious foreigners. And the head of the Secret Service stared nervously at the sky, watching for suspicious aircraft . . . .

The West Coast was in a state of panic. In Los Angeles an anti-aircraft battery blasted away at enemy bombers that were not there. In San Francisco an Army General swore that he saw a flock of 15 enemy planes buzzing the city. In Seattle authorities ordered all lights extinguished to fool [terrorist] pilots, and mobs enforced the blackout by smashing store windows that had been left illuminated—and looting the stores. America was paralyzed by fear and panic.[87]

The date was December 7, 1941—"Pearl Harbor Day," the day that Franklin D. Roosevelt declared "will live in infamy." By the time the smoke had cleared that Sunday, 19 American warships and 118 American aircraft had been destroyed, and 2,330 American soldiers and sailors were dead or dying. Tens of millions of men, women, and children—military and civilian—would give up their lives before the war ended.

"It had been a fine, golden autumn," the historian William Manchester would later write of that Fall of 1941 in New England, "a lovely farewell to those who would lose their youth and some of them their lives before the leaves turned again in a peacetime fall."

But the war effort was not Manchester's "fine golden Autumn." For Americans, the war was an "unnecessary necessity."[88] We did not start it, but we could not let it continue. It was necessary because, for most Americans, there was no other way to stop the carnage and despotism than bloody slaughter and immeasurable sacrifice. But, like all wars, it was tragically unnecessary. War is always the tragic failure of peace.

Sixty years later, in yet another war, we are still moved to patriotism, to flag waving, to public prayers for victory, to donating blood, sweat, and tears. Many of us are still stunned in a state of shock. But there are no compelling challenges to refocus our passions this time: no scrap metal drives, no driving door-to-door to collect discarded utensils and tools to feed the blast furnaces of war, no war bonds, or victory gardens, or rationed sugar, gas, and shoes, no massive employment of women in factories and defense communication centers, no civil defense drills or bomb shelters.

Like one young woman said recently, "My personal concerns seem so trivial, compared to what has happened. But I have no idea what I can do." It is about time that we realize that our country was wrong in not appealing to the very best in Americans: our willingness to sacrifice for the good of our nation. Instead, we were encouraged by our government to spend more in our consumerism. The great national call to sacrifice after September 11 was to "go shopping."

There was a better way but we chose not to follow it. In the midst of our anger, fear, frustration, and helplessness, we could have discovered within ourselves, our families, our communities, our churches, synagogues and mosques, our communities, and our nation a new strength of resolve and a dedication to make the world a better place. As Franklin Delano Roosevelt put it in 1941,

> *"In times like these we must all be reminded*
> *of who we really are . . .*
> *We will not give up . . .*
> *We will not give in."*

In the Biblical vision, the disorder and chaos that exist in all of creation is reversed: wolf and lamb, leopard and kid, lion and fatling, cow and bear, lion and ox, infant and asp are at peace. No more war and destruction. No more childless parents and parentless children. All anger, division, and violence will come to an end in the reign of a Spirit-filled Son of David. And all the earth will come to know the greatness and goodness of God.

2,800 years later we are still looking for a national leader with the wisdom of Solomon and the strength and humility of David.

Clearly, the lion is not yet lying down with the lamb, and the earth has not recognized the greatness and goodness of God.

Yet, in another sense, the promise has been fulfilled. In the coming of Jesus the disorder of Eden has been ordered aright; Satan is rejected; the savagery has been overcome in one human person.

In Isaiah 11, the prophet pictures a devastated forest, hacked down by God, stumps dotting the landscape, wood scattered helter-skelter, eerily silent—until the wind blows and a small shoot from a stump reaches skyward out of the devastation, like a blade of green grass thrusting skyward in the rubble of Ground Zero.

"Peacemaking starts every time you move out of the house of fear and into the house of love," claimed Henri Nouwen. He defined three characteristics of a personal spirituality of peacemaking: first, a prayer life which brings individuals into communion with God and with one another; second, resistance to the forces of fear, death, and prejudice; and third, a life in community. "We are not God," he declared, "but we can be mediators in a limited way of the unlimited love of God."

The major task of the church is rather to be the embodiment of a creation that will make it unnecessary for people to leave one another bleeding in the first place.

In November of 2001, a vast array of American religious leaders issued a public response to terrorism entitled, "DENY THEM THEIR VICTORY." They declared, "We share the deep anger toward those who so callously and massively destroy innocent lives, no matter what the grievances or injustices invoked. In the name of God, we too demand that those responsible for these utterly evil acts be found and brought to justice. . . . But we must not, out of anger and vengeance, indiscriminately retaliate in ways that bring on even more loss of innocent life. . . .

"The terrorists have offered us a stark view of the world they would create, where the remedy to every human grievance and injustice is a resort to the random and cowardly violence of revenge—even against the most innocent. Having taken thousands of our lives, attacked our national symbols, forced our political leaders to flee their chambers of governance, disrupted our work and families, and struck fear into the hearts of our children, the terrorists must feel victorious. BUT WE CAN DENY THEM THEIR VICTORY BY REFUSING TO SUBMIT TO A WORLD CREATED IN THEIR IMAGE . . . .

"We must not allow this terror to drive us away from being the people God has called us to be. We assert the vision of community, tolerance, compassion, justice, and the sacredness of human life, which lies at the heart of all our religious traditions. . . . Let us make the right choices in this crisis—to pray, act, and unite against the bitter fruits of division, hatred, and violence. Let us rededicate ourselves to global peace, human dignity, and the eradication of injustice that breeds rage and violence. AS WE GATHER IN OUR HOUSES OF WORSHIP, LET US BEGIN A PROCESS OF SEEKING THE HEALING AND GRACE OF GOD."[89]

Some six centuries before our planet was photographed from outer space, an English mystic known as Julian of Norwich described a similar vision of the earth's precariousness. "And in this vision," she wrote, "[Jesus] showed me a little thing, the size of a hazelnut, lying in the palm of my hand, and to my mind's eyes it was as round as any ball. I looked at it and thought, 'What can this be?' And the answer came to me, 'It is all that is made.' I wondered how it could last, for it was so small I thought it might suddenly disappear. And the answer to my mind was, 'It lasts and will last for ever because God loves it. . . .'"

The cynic's question, of course, is, "If God loves that little hazelnut-sized creation so much, then why does God put it Julian's hands?" But, if Mother Julian is telling the truth, it would seem that the answer is that God has faith in human beings like you and me. The only question is: "Will we prove worthy of God's faith?"

Our parents may not have been "The Greatest Generation." Every generation gives birth to great people with noble ambitions. But what made their generation great was their willingness to set aside their private pursuits for the general welfare of the nation. When duty called, they could be counted on to respond. When there was a choice to be made between private pleasures and public responsibility, they chose to sacrifice for the common good. Because of that choice, many of them are not here today to cheer us on. Many of them lost their lives and fortunes, but they gained for us a future. They may not have had much, but they had each other, and that was enough. Can we do any less than they in our recommitment to our families, our religious communities, our nation, and our world?

At the height of World War II, Winston Churchill asked a struggling nation, "What is the use of living if you cannot leave the world a better place because you were there?"

America is not about buying and flying, using and abusing, hoarding and controlling the earth. America is too good for that. And she will not last long if she judges her true wealth by those criteria.

I believe that we can once again respond to the call of duty and prove ourselves grateful of God's love in Christ and worthy of God's faith in us.

"Come, my friends," wrote Tennyson, "'tis not too late to seek a newer world."

CHAPTER 15

THE MYSTIC CHORDS OF MEMORY

"A king is not saved by his great army;
a warrior is not delivered by his great strength.
The war horse is a vain hope for victory,
and by its great might it cannot save."
—PSALM 33:16, 17

On March 4, 1861, in his First Inaugural Address, President Abraham Lincoln pleaded with a divided nation: "We are not enemies, but friends. We must not be enemies. Though passion may have strained, it must not break our bonds of affection. The mystic chords of memory, stretching from every battlefield and patriot grave to every living heart and hearthstone all over this broad land, will yet swell the chorus of the Union when again touched, as surely they will be, by the better angels of our nature."

Tragically, the chorus of the Union was not sufficiently touched by those "better angels."

Seven years and nearly a million deaths later, on May 5, 1868, John A. Logan, Commander-in-Chief of the Grand Army of the Republic, issued a general order designating May 30, 1868, as a day "for the purpose of strewing with flowers or otherwise decorating the graves of comrades who died in defense of their country during the late rebellion." He went on to say that he did this "with the hope that this memorial will be kept up from year to year."

If not Lincoln's, at least the General's hope has been fulfilled. Calling it first "Decoration" and then "Memorial" Day, for 141 years we Americans have strewn with flowers the graves of comrades fallen in the Civil and subsequent wars, graves of those "who will not grow old as we who are left grow old."

Each year this grateful nation remembers its patriots who answered the call of duty and made the ultimate sacrifice for their country, be it during the Civil War, the Great War, the Second World War, Korea, Vietnam, the Gulf War, the Iraq War, or countless other wars declared and undeclared.

Like the people of Israel of old who crossed over the Jordan River into the Land of Promise, out of slavery and wandering into promise and hope, we still mark our national memories with memorial stones. In order that later, when the generations who follow ask the question, "What do these stones mean to you?" our children will be able to answer. But what will they say?

"A man's real possession is his memory," it has been said.

"In nothing else is he rich, in nothing else is he poor."[90] Our memories can be our greatest blessings and our greatest curses.

As the Queen remarked in Lewis Carroll's *Through the Looking Glass*, "It's a poor sort of memory that works only backwards."

T.S. Eliot reminds us, there are always those

> *"Footfalls (which) echo in the memory*
> *Down the passage which we did not take*
> *Towards the door we never opened*
> *Into the Rose-garden.*[91]

Each year on Memorial Day we temporarily set aside our institutional structures and the historical accidents which caused our religious breaks from one another so long ago. On this day we celebrate the in-breaking of the Spirit on that day when our ancestors were dramatically invited into the possibilities of a new community of faith beyond tribal conflicts—without being asked to do the impossible: to forget their stories, abandon their homes, or step out of their traditions.

Rather, they were called to a higher loyalty than race or gender, clan or nation, and empowered with a stronger Spirit than mere survival or self-interest. Although their passions had been strained, their bonds of affection were not broken. Those "mystic chords of memory" were touched in that Upper Room by the "better angels of their nature."

I believe that our passions, loyalties, and bonds of affection can again be touched by the fires of love and the tongues of courage. When that happens, our children will be able to say that those memory stones of war helped them remember not only the worst, but the best of humanity. War has taught millions to care for and share with one another as though their lives depended upon it—which it did. Soldiers have shared more hopes and fears in an hour in a foxhole than most people do in a lifetime.

People go to war for their ideal, but they die for each other, for their friends and comrades, and/or the people back home who

love them. What my stepfather, as well as my father-in-law, re-
called most vividly about the war were not primarily events, but
themselves under pressure, their own selves that were better, more
courageous, more caring. As the citation on one Celtic Cross says,
"Courage Disdains Fame and Wins It."

And so on each Veteran's Day we thank those of you who risked
your own death for the sake of our lives and our children. We
salute you.

It is a humbling thing to be died for. It is not just comrades and
buddies and friends who have been died for. But also we who are
alive today because of others' sacrifice.

We can be nostalgic about the old ways of the past. But let us
not repeat them. Let us not glorify war or the horrors of killing.
Remembrance is about "re-membering," putting back together,
not "dismembering," as tens of thousands of children maimed and
killed each year by land mines from old wars remind us. Those
whom we honor on Memorial Day died bravely to protect innocent lives. Is it too much to suggest that we all should live to do
no less?

Wars do not kill children, people do. And political ideologies do
not save children, people do. In this global-village world, war is no
longer the answer. With our current stockpiles of nuclear weapons
already able to kill every living thing on earth several times over,
we must say "NO" to nuclear weapon production, and "YES" to
the total elimination of nuclear weapons on the earth. None of us
is safe as long as any of us can kill the rest of us.

"Either [humanity] is obsolete or war is."[92]

We are the first generation free enough to stand on the shoulders of those gone before us and see further than they—to envision a world beyond war. We dare not fail in this sacred trust.

President and General Dwight D. Eisenhower, no stranger to the
battlefield, said it passionately:

"People in the long run are going to do more to promote peace
than governments. Indeed, I think that people want peace so
much that one of these days governments had better get out of

their way and let them have it. . . . Every gun that is made, every warship launched, every rocket fired, signifies a theft from those who hunger and are not fed, those who are cold and are not clothed. The world in arms is not spending money alone. It is spending the sweat of its laborers, the genius of its scientists, and the hopes of its children. This is not a way of life at all in any true sense. Under the cloud of war, it is humanity hanging on a cross of iron."[93]

What will our children say of these stones?

My friends, I have great confidence in the spirit of America, touched by "the better angels of our nature." I believe that, in spite of the selfishness of some, the majority of people in this country will refuse to let our own people die of poverty and the world's people die of war. With de Toqueville, I believe that "America is great because America is good. If she ceases to be good, she ceases to be great."[94]

And with Carl Sandburg, "I see America, not in the setting sun of a black night of despair ahead of us. I see America in the crimson light of a rising sun fresh from the burning, creative handoff God. I see great days ahead, great days possible to men and women of vision."[95]

We owe our war heroes something beyond our gratitude on Memorial Day. We owe them the assurance that their deaths were not in vain. We owe them what thy fought and died for: their country at peace with itself and with the world.

When that happens, the whole earth shall be their memorial

> "The tumult and the shouting dies;
>   The captains and the kings depart;
> Still stands Thine ancient sacrifice,
>   A humble and a contrite heart.
> Lord God of Hosts, be with us yet,
> Lest we forget—lest we forget!"[96]

CHAPTER 16

DARE WE HOPE AGAIN?

(A Dialogue Between
Mikhail Gorbachev and Barack Obama)

Author and Columnist James Carroll recently wrote in The Boston Globe: "Twenty years ago this month, Mikhail Gorbachev stood before the UN General Assembly and said, 'The compelling necessity of freedom of choice is also clear to us. The failure to recognize this . . . is fraught with very dire consequences, consequences for world peace.' At that time, as Soviet General Secretary, Gorbachev was the ruler of hundreds of millions of people, both in the Soviet Union and in Central and Eastern Europe—a population that had no freedom of choice. The government over which Gorbachev presided had long made sure that was the case. Freedom of choice would get you killed. That is why his declaration stunned the world. 'Freedom of choice is a universal principle to which there should be no exceptions. . . .'

"All of this, Gorbachev said, was 'aimed at the demilitarization of international relations,' the changing of the world economy 'from an economy of armament to an economy of disarmament,' and 'the movement toward a nuclear-free and nonviolent world.' He saluted Ronald Reagan, whose term was just ending, and with whom he had already agreed in principle to abolish nuclear weapons . . .

"The 'decisive year' for which Gorbachev called two decades ago may now be here—for our side. Americans stand today, as the last Soviet dictator put it then, 'on the threshold of a year from which all of us expect so much. One would like to believe that our joint efforts to put an end to the era of wars, confrontation and regional conflicts, aggression against nature, the terror of hunger and poverty, as well as political terrorism, will be comparable with our hopes.'

"Is it too much to expect Barack Obama to change history? Make peace? Transform an economic system? Rescue the Earth? Build a political program around the truth? Restore a great nation's decency? Are we kidding ourselves to place such hopes in him?"[97]

"Hope in the face of difficulty, hope in the face of uncertainty, the audacity of hope!

In the end, that is God's greatest gift to us, the bedrock of this nation, a belief in things not seen, a belief that there are better days ahead. . . .

In the face of impossible odds, people who love their country can change it."
—BARACK OBAMA [98]

"On the cusp of this decisive year," writes Carroll, "it will do Americans well to recall that just such a transformation took place once before, even if we declined to respond with transformation of our own. By the grace of God, it is not too late to match the greatness with which Gorbachev acted 20 years ago, an overdue acceptance of his historic invitation. 'This is our common goal,' he concluded, 'and it is only by acting together that we may attain it.'"[99]

Rising to the occasion, Barack Obama, President of the United States, reminded us: "This is your victory . . . we proved once more that the true strength of our nation comes not from the might of our arms or the scale of our wealth, but from the enduring power of our ideals."[100]

"On this [Inauguration] day, we gather because we have chosen hope over fear, unity of purpose over conflict and discord. . . . We remain a young nation, but in the words of Scripture, the time has come to set aside childish things. The time has come to reaffirm our enduring spirit; to choose our better history; to carry forward that precious gift, that noble idea, passed on from generation to generation: the God-given promise that all are equal, all are free, and all deserve a chance to pursue their full measure of happiness. . . . With old friends and former foes, we will work tirelessly to lessen the nuclear threat [and to those who] seek to advance their aims by inducing terror and slaughtering innocents, we say to you know that our spirit is stronger and cannot be broken; you cannot outlast us, and we will defeat you. . . .

"Let it be told to the future world . . . that in the depth of winter, when nothing but hope and virtue could survive . . . that the city and the country, alarmed at one common danger, came forth to meet [it]. . . .

"In the face of our common dangers, in this winter of our hardships, let us remember these timeless words. With hope and virtue, let us brave once more the icy currents, and endure what storms may come. Let it be said by our children's children that when we were tested we refused to let this journey end, that we did not turn back nor did we falter; and with eyes fixed one the horizon and God's grace upon us, we carried forth that great gift of freedom and delivered its safely to future generations."[101]

Dare we hope again? How can we not? How can we not follow "the angels of our better nature" and hope again? "We must accept finite disappointment . . ." as Martin Luther King put it, "but we must never lose infinite hope."

"Not everything that is faced can be changed. But nothing can be changed until it is faced."[102]

BISHOP V. GENE ROBINSON'S INVOCATION AT THE INAUGURAL OPENING CEREMONY JANUARY 20, 2009

Please join me in pausing for a moment, to ask God's blessing upon our nation and our next president.

O God of our many understandings, we pray that you will bless us with tears—tears for a world in which over a billion people exist on less than a dollar a day, where young women in many lands are beaten and raped for wanting an education, and thousands die daily from malnutrition, malaria, and AIDS.

Bless this nation with anger—anger at discrimination, at home and abroad, against refugees and immigrants, women, people of color, gay, lesbian, bisexual, and transgender people.

Bless us with discomfort at the easy, simplistic answers we've preferred to hear from our politicians, instead of the truth about ourselves and our world, which we need to face if we are going to rise to the challenges of the future.

Bless us with patience and the knowledge that none of what ails us will be fixed anytime soon, and the understanding that our new president is a human being, not a messiah.

Bless us with humility, open to understanding that our own needs as a nation must always be balanced with those of the world.

Bless us with freedom from mere tolerance, replacing it with a genuine respect and warm embrace of our differences.

Bless us with compassion and generosity, remembering that every religion's God judges us by the way we care for the most vulnerable.

And God, we give you thanks for your child, Barack, as he assumes the office of President of the United States.

Give him wisdom beyond his years, inspire him with President

Lincoln's reconciling leadership style, President Kennedy's ability to enlist our best efforts, and Dr. King's dream of a nation for all people.

Give him a quiet heart, for our ship of state needs a steady, calm captain.

Give him stirring words; we will need to be inspired and motivated to make the personal and common sacrifices necessary to facing the challenges ahead.

Make him color-blind, reminding him of his own words that under his leadership, there will be neither red nor blue states, but the United States.

Help him remember his own oppression as a minority, drawing on that experience of discrimination, that he might seek to change the lives of those who are still its victims.

Give him strength to find family time and privacy, and help him remember that even though he is president, a father only gets one shot at his daughters' childhoods.

And please, God, keep him safe. We know we ask too much of our presidents, and we're asking far too much of this one. We implore you, O good and great God, to keep him safe. Hold him in the palm of your hand, that he might do the work we have called him to do, that he might find joy in this impossible calling, and that in the end, he might lead us as a nation to a place of integrity, prosperity, and peace. **Amen.**

HOPE FOR LIFE

CHAPTER 17

HOPE SPRINGS ETERNAL

Christians attend church for different reasons. Especially on Easter Sunday. But it makes no difference the reason. "Like the swallows who know when to return to Capistrano, like the [salmon] who know when to swim upstream and against the current, and like the buds and bulbs who know when to break out of their [tombs] and burst forth, you know that on this day, above all others, this is the place, above all others, where you are meant to be."[103]

For Christians, "Easter is the New Year's Day of the soul!"[104]

There is in the human heart a yearning for significance, a dream that life is more than we have yet experienced, a hope that life will ultimately win out over death, and that love will outlast it all.

As Alexander Pope put it,

> *"Hope springs eternal in the human breast:*
> *Man never is, but always to be blest."*[105]

What does it all mean, this life of ours? Bill Moyers asked the question some years ago of the great philosopher Joseph Campbell. Campbell replied, "That is the wrong question! We are not looking for the meaning of life, we are looking for the experience of being alive, which the quest for meaning wipes out."

That is the message of Easter. Heralded from an empty tomb in the side of a nondescript mountain to nothing less than terrified disciples comes the everlasting affirmation: "Why do you look for the living among the dead? He is not here, but [he] has risen."[106]

Try as we might to make some sense out of the absurdities and atrocities of life to derive some meaning out of

- the tombs that hold the dead hopes and dreams of nations,
- the dwindling expectations of churches, synagogues, and mosques,
- the painful yearnings of families, relatives, and friends, and
- the countless futures broken by violence, betrayal, and indifference . . .

We will not find our answers to life's meaning there in the darkness of the grave.

The voices from the tombs echo through the centuries: "Why do you look for the living among the dead?" "Why do you look for the meaning of life in the tragedy of life?" The message of Easter is that life is found, not in the fruitless search for reasons, but in the experience of being alive.

Maybe we are looking for love in all the wrong places.

Many of us have spent too long in the darkness of an empty tomb. We have cried too long in the dark and demanded to know "Why?" in the shadows. What we have lost is gone. What we have demanded to know is unknowable.

We have but one choice: to stay in the darkness of the tomb, or to turn toward the light of the new day. The only way out of the darkness is to follow the risen Christ into the light.

"Consider the tombs where hopes and possibilities in your life have been wrapped in linen and hidden away forever behind a stone. Brave wondering about a broken dream of these recent days lying in the darkness as you, perhaps, secretly mourn. Even in the darkness, return to the tomb that holds your dead yearning. Find the stone rolled away. Look inside. . . . Pay attention to what the mystery is trying to tell you.

"Now turn around. Meet the stranger.

"Who or what is it that you see but do not recognize when you turn from the tomb?

"Tell him why you weep and all you have lost.

"Hear him call you by name.

"When you reach out to hold him [and he refuses] . . . what do you discover about holding onto and letting go that is the first step toward embracing new life?

"Hear him say instead to go to the others and tell them what is happening."[107]

Life's greatest longings are not realized in the historicity of the facts of an empty tomb. The deep questions of life are not answered by a man-made creed, nor by a classic doctrine of the church. As many of you know, Paul was the earliest New Testament writer, within a generation of Jesus. And it is clear that his resurrection faith, like the faith of the disciples, was not based on the negative argument of an empty tomb, but on the positive conviction that the Lord had appeared to him.

The great question of Easter is not: "Who rolled away the stone?" but rather, "Have you encountered a Risen Christ? Have you been touched by an Everlasting Love?"

That post-Easter Christ says to us, as to Mary, "Don't cling to me! Follow me. I will meet you in the future, not in the past." There is no going back. Jesus is not there. Our hope is not found in our ability to hold onto him, but in his ability to hold onto us. Maybe we need to let go of Jesus in order to let Jesus take hold of us. One writer wrestles with the pain of doing this:

"I have never been able to positively let go of anyone or anything I really loved. Instead, things, people, self-images, god-images, and dreams have been taken away from me. And most of them . . . have been left covered with [my] claw marks. Letting go is not a positive, assertive action. Instead, we can only chose to allow it to happen when—and only when—grace invites and empowers it. . . . The 'doing' of letting go is nothing more than a soft, gentle response, a tenderly-whispered YES to an invitation and a possibility offered from somewhere beyond our own wills."[108]

Mary called him "Rabbouni!" But that was his Friday name. But then Sunday came, and his name is Emmanuel, "God With Us." And he is not content to stop with us. He is on his way back to God and is taking the whole world with him.

Resurrection does not mean resuscitation, going back to the old life. Resurrection means re-creation, *ex-nihilo*, dying completely and then being recreated anew out of nothing. Resurrection means life bursting forth out of nothingness—even the nothingness of loss. The empty tomb trumpets the ultimate Alleluia—that love, compassion, generosity, humility, selflessness, and hope will ultimately triumph over suffering, hatred, bigotry, prejudice, despair, greed, and death.

The Fetchet family in our town of New Canaan, Connecticut, discovered something of the reality of Easter hope after their son Brad's death in the horror of the World Trade Center tragedy. In the midst of the hell of nothingness and loss, Mary, Frank, Wes, and Chris found solace not only in their community of family and friends, but in their faith. They have encouraged me to share with you their favorite poem, attributed to St. Francis deSales:

> *"Do not look forward in fear to the changes in life;*
> *rather look to them with full hope that as they arise,*
> *God, whose very own you are,*
> *Will lead you safely through all things.*
> *And when you cannot stand it,*
> *You will be carried in God's arms.*
> *Do not fear what may happen tomorrow;*
> *The same everlasting God who cares for you today*
> *Will take care of you then and every day.*
> *God will either shield you from suffering*
> *Or will give you unfailing strength to bear it.*
> *Be at peace and put aside all anxious thoughts*
> *and imaginations."*[109]

My friends, we have enough people in the world who tell it like it is; we could use a few who tell it like it can be. The tomb is open on Easter morning; but our hope is not there, in the darkness. It is here, in the light.

On Easter Morning . . . we who have been crushed by broken hopes and broken dreams and broken relationships can dare to hope again.

On Easter Morning . . . we who have been laid low by illness and hampered by the frailties of our bodies can rise in spirit over our infirmities.

On Easter Morning . . . we who have suffered the hell of losing a loved one and part of ourselves can be loved back to life by the Source of all Love.

On Easter Morning . . . we who have become callused and cynical in the boredom and despair of our meaningless lives can regain our lost passion for life.

On Easter Morning . . . we who have cried and prayed and worked for peace and justice, only to see it dashed on the rocks of selfish gain and godless power, can believe again that, in the end, love will win.

The resurrection of Christ is nothing short of "a cosmic victory of seemingly powerless love over loveless power."[110] It happened once. It can happen again. It will happen again. It is happening again.

Because of Easter turn with me away from the darkness of the empty tomb, toward the light of a new day and a new hope. When you leave the sanctuary of your choosing this next Easter, envision leaving behind all the excess baggage you brought with you, all of that stuff that draws you down to death. Let it go. Then turn from the darkness of death into the light of a new day and a new hope. The Lord has gone ahead of you. You will meet him in the future, not the past. For "he is not here, he has risen."

Then it will be true, as we sing throughout the world each Easter morning,

> *"Made like him, like him we rise,*
> *Ours the cross, the grave, the skies."*

Thanks be to God. **Amen.**

THE BEST OF MY DAYS

In Tibetan Buddhism, the word "shul" means the impression left when something has passed through. A cave carved out by water. A footprint in the mud. The enormous white space that opens when you stop clinging to what you think will protect you, whether it's love or success. The unguarded void that remains when you realize you're mortal, the clearing into which insight can move and some other voice can be heard.

We need, it seems, some absence in order to feel the presence of something larger. Monks use the word "shul" to mean the holy path of emptiness they travel. And in Yiddish, the word means "temple."

Your life and mine each need our "shuls," our quiet intimations of mortality, our places of emptiness into which the presence of the Spirit can make its abode.

Tragically, we continue to race through life rather than letting life fill us. "Getting and spending we lay waste our power. Little we see in nature which is ours."[111]

Yet, as Bill Coffin would often put it, "It is by its content, rather than its duration, that a life is measured."

Recently Dr. Karen Steinhauser and her colleagues at the Veterans Affairs Medical Center in Durham, North Carolina, released the results of their clinical study of the crucial components of a "good death" and of a "bad death." A "bad death," as they term it, exists when patients feel disregarded, family members feel perplexed, and care providers feel out of control. The first three elements of a good death are proactive: Pain and Symptom Management, Clear Decision-Making, and Preparation for Death. The final three are more life-encompassing, like the Buddhists' open space for life's embrace:

Completion. Reviewing one's life, resolving conflicts, spending time with family and friends, and saying good-bye;

Contribution to Others. Achieving a clarity as to what is really important in life and wanting to share that understanding with others.

And finally, Affirmation. An individual in his or her final days of life wants to be seen as a unique and whole person, and to be understood in the context of their life, values and preferences.[112]

This seems like such a healthy approach to death, doesn't it? So much healthier than denying it, or getting stuck in anger, or bargaining, or depression, before we finally accept our own death.[113]

I suggest that these last three elements of a "good death" are also the essentials for a "good life." What if every day we took a time-out to review our life, resolve the conflicts of the day, and spend time with family and friends? My hunch is that such a simple formula would help us achieve certain clarity about our life—which we would want to share with others. I believe that living such a life each day would provide us with a centeredness as a unique and whole person, so that our final days would be more serene and gracious as we prepare ourselves for the next step in life.

It is not that we need to live long. It is that we need to live well. What better epigraph could there be than, "She lived her life well"?

Having sat at the bedside of hundreds of friends in their final moments, I can tell you that toward the end there is often a visceral experience of peace in their eyes, and a palpable feeling of calm throughout their bodies—especially when they have come to terms with their mortality and have accepted the completion of their life, found a clarity of what is truly important in life, and have been affirmed as a unique and valuable person.

How can you and I get to that point of inner-calm, of self-acceptance and peace before it's too late? This is where religion comes into play. Forrest Church, former minister of the All Soul's Unitarian Church in New York City, embraced a wonderful definition of religion in the final years of his struggle with cancer: *"Religion is our human response to the dual reality of being alive and knowing we must die.* We are not so much the animal with tools or the animal with advanced language as we are the religious animal. Knowing we must one day die, we cannot help but question what life means. . . . We seek meaning in life, not the meaning of life.

. . . The purpose of life and its truest test as well, is to live in such a way that our lives will prove worth dying for."

"So, whenever a trap door swings or the roof caves in, don't ask, 'Why?' Why will get you nowhere. The only question worth asking is, 'Where do we go from here?' And part of the answer must be, 'together.' Together we kneel. Together we walk, holding one another's hands, holding each other up. Together we do love's work and thereby we are saved."[114]

In his book, *Beyond the Mirror*, Henri Nouwen reflects on death during his recovery from a near-lethal accident. "The very simple truth," he writes, "is that the way in which I die affects many people. If I die with much anger and bitterness, I will leave my family and friends behind in confusion, guilt, shame, or weakness. When I felt my death approaching, I suddenly realized how much I could influence the hearts of those whom I would leave behind. If I could truly say that I was grateful for what I had lived, eager to forgive and be forgiven, full of hope that those who loved me would continue their lives in joy and peace, and confident that Jesus who calls me would guide all who somehow had belonged to my life—if I could do that—I would, in the hour of my death, reveal more true spiritual freedom than I had been able to reveal during all the years of my life. I realized on a very deep level that dying is the most important act of living. It involves a choice to bind others with guilt or to set them free with gratitude. This choice is a choice between a death that gives life and a death that kills. . . ."[115]

This is why we choose to join together in our houses of worship rather than remain in the privacy of our own homes, or in the lostness of a crowd, simply because experience has taught us that we need one another.

"We need guidance in recognizing our tears in one another's eyes. We need prompting to raise our moral sights. We need companions in the work of love and justice to enhance our neighborhoods and to strengthen our witness in the world. And yes, we choose to join our hands and hearts because we know how easily we slip back into mechanical habits that blunt our consciousness. We know we need to be reminded week in and week out how precious life is and how fragile. So very fragile. And so phosphorescent. A year can seem to last forever, to the point that we may pray for it to end; yet decades flit past in an eye blink."[116]

As so many of you, Bev and I have each been thrust into the reality of this with the cruel and untimely deaths of each of our brothers. Their lives seemed so short. And our time with them so brief. Yet there was so much good in their living that we are learning how to let them go on.

As people of faith, we know that each of our lives come from God, and that each of our lives will return to God. And we know that the resurrection of Christ symbolizes for us the power of God in triumph over the power of death. Death is a horizon, and a horizon is nothing save the limit of our sight. So, the issue for us is not how we will be in heaven, but rather, how we will be on earth. How we live our lives against the backdrop of our deaths will determine whether ours will be a "good death."

How do you and I wish to be remembered when our lives are completed? Have we done all we can do? Have we said all we can say? Have we been all we can be? Have we loved all we can love? Have we laughed all we can laugh? Will our well-lived lives light the way for our own children . . . and for our children's children . . . and for so many others who will follow us on this beautiful and precarious planet.

As E. E. Cummings voiced it:

> "i thank you God for most this amazing
> day: for the leaping greenly spirits of trees
> and a blue true dream of sky; and for everything
> which is natural, which is infinite, which is yes
>
> (i who have died am alive again today,
> and this is the sun's birthday; this is the birth
> day of life and love and wings: and of the gay
> great happening illimitably earth) . . .

(now the ears of my ears awake and
now the eyes of my eyes are opened)

In closing, I share with you a beautiful Muslim prayer which speaks so eloquently and simply:

"O Lord, may the end of my life be the best of it;
may my closing acts be my best acts;
and may the best of my days
be the day when I shall meet Thee."

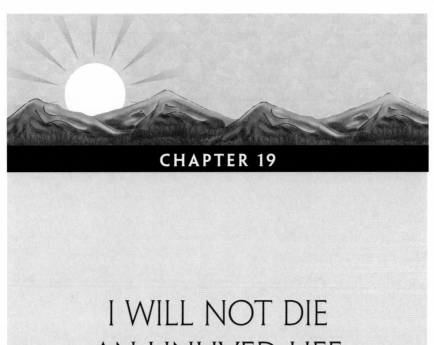

I WILL NOT DIE
AN UNLIVED LIFE

Dawna was lying on the operating table in a Boston hospital. Or her body was. She heard the doctor yell to the nurse, "Damn! We lost her. Adrenaline stat!"

As she tells it, she would have preferred hearing a Mozart concerto, or Maya Angelou reciting "And Still I Rise" in a hot whisper in her ear. Even a cat purring would have been nice. But the doctor yelling was the last thing she heard.

"A drop of rain falls into the ocean and becomes part of a swelling wave. Imagine you are the raindrop. A hand grabs so tightly onto something for decades that it becomes numb, then finally, it just opens, releases with a sigh. Imagine you are the hand. Imagine the safest experience you could ever know." That is how she describes her dying.

"People have asked me if I saw The Light. I have to tell the truth. My experience was more like bending toward light. It was like being stained with light.

"And since every truth must balance with another, I also experienced a pervasive darkness. Not hellfire. But the awareness of how the soul's great capacity for love, the love that had been leaking out of my life for so long was excruciating. To know how incomplete my loving had been was agonizing—how I had limited it with all my stories that loving was a thing, a commodity I could 'give' or not, had earned or not. . . .

"There was a conversation, a dialogue without words, between my soul and the life I had lived. It took place in a complete white silence, and was more subtle than thought, more like the whispering between a tree and the wind blowing through it.

"'Have you had enough joy?' it asked.

"Enough joy?" she thought. "I haven't even begun to live and now I've died!"

"'Well, what have you been waiting for?'

"'What's unfinished for you to give?' the voice whispered.

"'What's unfinished for you to heal?'

"'What's unfinished for you to learn?'

"'What's unfinished for you to experience?'

"What could I say? These questions did not demand answers. They required only that I open to them. I felt, in essence, my mind wanting to learn the way a seed wants to swell and sprout, my soul wanting to experience the way an apple branch wants to blossom, my heart wanting to give extravagantly the way a blossom wants to fruit.

"Have you ever fallen asleep and then awakened with a start so that your body literally jumps?" she asks. "I fell back into my body, which was being wheeled on a gurney to the morgue. I would say not that I, who had never failed a test, flunked dying— except that I slammed into my body with the stunning awareness that death is not a failure."[117]

That is the way Dawna Markova describes her experience of dying some thirty years ago. In her autobiography, she contrasts her experience with that of her father. "He died with a shrug," she says, "His heart was hollow and vacant of dreams," she says. "He was convinced he didn't matter."

When her mother told her that her father had just passed away, she wept herself asleep. Even though he beat her when she was a child, she ached with sadness. "The tears broke through me the way the frozen rivers in Vermont break open in the spring. Rivers of reaching, rivers of yearning. I floated to sleep on a surging tide of grief."

She awakened with a renewed passion for life. She picked up her pen and wrote this:

> *"I will not die an unlived life.*
> *I will not live in fear*
> *of falling or catching fire.*
> *I choose to inhabit my days,*
> *to allow my living to open me,*
> *to make me less afraid,*
> *more accessible,*
> *to loosen my heart*
> *until it becomes a wing,*

a torch, a promise.
I choose to risk my significance,
To live so that which came to me as seed
Goes to the next as blossom,
and that which came to me as blossom,
goes on as fruit."[118]

That is how Dawna Markova expresses her personal dedication to living each day of her life as if it were the last.

Your experience and mine may be nothing like Dawna's near death encounter and her inspired poetry the night her father died. But is there not a sense in which the stuff of all of our life stories is wrapped up in the same struggle to find some meaning, some life, some joy and contribution out of our few days on the earth? "Each of us is here to give something that only we can offer, and when we avoid knowing ourselves, we end up living numb, passionless lives, disconnected from our soul's true purpose. But when you have the courage to shape your life from the essence of who you are, you ignite, becoming truly alive."[119]

In Boris Pasternak's epic novel, Doctor Zhivago declares, "Man is born to live, not to prepare to live."

That has been the driving force in my life over the years. The Christian Life is about this life, not the next. Yes, the Bible witnesses to a life beyond this one. For us as Christians, Jesus' death and resurrection open up a new world of reality beyond the present. We are right to sing our tributes "to all the saints, from whom their labors rest." But traditional Christianity has put so much emphasis on the next life (of which we know little, if anything), that the significance of fully living this life (the only one we know) has been negated.

The "unexamined life," as Socrates put it, may not be worth living. But the "unlived life" is not worth examining. We need to rediscover the "his worldliness" of the Gospel. Our Lord Jesus came "that we might have life, and have it abundantly."[120] Not just eternal life, but everyday, common life, lived passionately to the glory of God.

Each of us has within us a natural life energy that pushes us, a deep and natural pulse that tells us to live from the inside out, to reach in and reach out for all that is possible to know, to contribute, and to receive.

In West Africa, there is a saying that it's the heart that lets go and the hands that follow. With Dawna, I am coming to understand that there is no such thing as "finding" one's purpose. It's about creating the conditions where your purpose can find you. It's not about asking what your life means. It's about being willing to receive the truth of what you hear.

What is the love that has been leaking out of your life for so long? What are your secret hopes? What is unfinished for you to give? What is unfinished for you to heal? What is unfinished for you to learn? What is unfinished for you to experience?

We can create the conditions in which a sense of our purpose can arise. But rarely can it be done alone. Most of the time we discover our passion for life and the powerful calling of our hearts in a safe, caring community of people who know us and love us. I'd like to think that churches are safe places where you can ask those questions personally and have your answers confirmed by others who know and love you. And then find there opportunities to put your passion into practice.

Do you remember the writings of Shutruk Nuhuntes in 1158 BC? Probably not . . . unless you watched the movie, "The Emperor's Club." Kevin Kline plays the role of a revered teacher in a New England boys' school. Above the door of his classroom is the inscription of this little-known ancient emperor, "King and Sovereign of the Land of Elan," which you cannot find in any history book: "NOBE SIBI"—NOT FOR ONESELF."

"Great ambition and conquest without contribution is without significance."

What will your contribution be: How will history remember you?

"To live in the hearts we leave behind is not to die."[121]

EPILOGUE

A LETTER TO MY GRANDDAUGHTERS

I would like to share with you a letter which I wrote to our first grand-child, Isabella Rose Wilburn when she was born, one month after the third anniversary of the tragic New York City September 11th Terrorist Attack in 2001. While it is written to her personally, it is also for her sister, Cameron Grace, born on February 23, 2007. I believe it echoes the concerns of every parent and grandparent in America today.

Dear Isabella and Cameron,

Twenty-four days ago a miracle happened. Isabella, out of the warm and silent darkness of your mother Joanie's womb, you exploded into light, kicking and screaming with life. Your father Sean was right there at your bedside to embrace you and your mom with his strong arms and large hands, while both of them cried as they held you close to their hearts. You were welcomed to life through unimaginable love . . . accompanied by

anxiety and ecstasy
tears and laughter,
sobs of pain and joy,
and uncontrollable convulsions of
expectation and fulfillment.

On Tuesday, the 7th of October, 2004, God chose to begin the world again, and give the earth another chance. And now again, on February 23, 2007, the world begins again with you, Cameron Grace.

Now the two of you, along with your mom and dad, have become our pioneers to lead the world into goodness and love.

> *"Every day is a fresh beginning;*
> *Listen my soul to the glad refrain.*
>
> *And, spite of old sorrows*
> *And older sinning;*
> *And puzzles forecasted,*
> *And possible pain,*
>
> *Take heart with the day*
> *And begin again."[122]*

Isabella and Cameron, you have been born into an expansive Family of Love reaching from California to New York, "from sea to shining sea." As we cradled your beautiful, precious little bodies in our arms, your Gramma Bev and I linked our hearts and prayers with your Nonna Joan, and have pledged to you and your parents that we will always be there for you.

Each of us knows that you are not only your parents' child, but are also a child of God, a daughter of Life's longing for itself. You have come through them, not just from them. And though they are your parents, you do not belong to them. You belong to the Universe:

to the open sky and the stars in their courses,
to clouds and rainbows,
to birdsong and butterflies,
to moonlight and firelight,
to the glisten of enthusiasm and a sense of wonder,
to a large hand reaching down for a small hand,
to long days to be merry in—and nights without fear.

Yet there is another side to this amazing new world of yours, Isabella and Cameron. At times this world can seem a cold and frightening place. Sometimes things happen that are very bad and are not God's will for any of us. Selfish and senseless cruelties happen all too often. Sometimes people hurt each other rather than help each other. Sometimes they forget that they are all members of the same big family all over the world. Sometimes they just think about themselves.

Your parents and so many other young couples in America have struggled about whether or not to bring new life into this sometimes scary world. But in love and not in fear, they have said "yes" to a new direction for the world. It is only through new life and new hope that the world will become less scary.

There are people in this world who live in very different conditions than we. It is much harder for some of them to be happy than it is for some of us. They think that their way is the only way, and try to force it on others. They become afraid for their families and their children. So they try to make other people afraid of them. They think that the only way they can be safe from being hurt is to hurt other people.

The world is a really big place. When you get older you will get to know more of its people. Most of them will be wonderful, loving, caring people. But a few of them will not be like that. There will be playmates who don't know how to play nicely and will try to make you cry. There will be bullies at your school who don't like themselves so they will not like you. And there will be some people in the world who don't like our country, or other countries, and will try to hurt us.

These are sad and angry people. Often their lives have been so hard that they have no hope for the future. Sometimes they see no reason to go on living. They no longer dream of better days. The only thing they think they have the power to do is to hurt other people.

What they hope is that we will be so scared of them that we will do whatever they say. They want you and your friends to grow up in a world where their way is the only way and fear is all that you can think about—a world in which fear controls your imagination, limits your horizons, and determines the laws by which you will live.

Sometimes being afraid is a good thing. It keeps us from running into the street in front of a car, or burning our hands on a hot stove. It keeps us from doing a lot of stupid things we might later regret.

But fear can also be a bad thing. The person who fears something gives that fear power over her. Fear makes the shadows move. Fear makes the boogeyman bigger than he really is. But there are very few monsters that deserve the fear we have of them. And Sadaam Hussein is not one of them. Nor is Osama Bin Laden. Too many people refuse to live their dreams because they insist on living their fears. Sometimes we become that which we are afraid of.

A lot of people will tell you that the most important day in the history of America, the day that defined who we are, was September 11, 2001. But it was not. The most important day in America was July 4, 1776, the Declaration of our Independence. "We hold these truths to be self-evident, that all men are created equal with certain inalienable Rights, that among these are Life, Liberty and the pursuit of Happiness. That to secure these rights, Governments are instituted among Men, deriving their just powers from the consent of the governed. . . . And for the support of this Declaration, with a firm reliance on the protection of divine Providence, we mutually pledge to each other our Lives, our Fortunes and our Sacred Honor. "

War is very scary, hon. But don't be afraid. There are lots of people out there watching out for us—like your grandfather Joe did so bravely. There are teachers and police and firefighters, the Army, Navy, Marines, Coast Guard, and National Guard.

But even more than that, God is trying to get the people of Iraq and the people of America and the other nations of the world to work together for the kind of human justice that can bring peace to all of us. The true God is bigger than any of our ideas about God.

Bigger and better . . . more kind and more caring. And that same God is in you and with you all day long and all night long. You will never be alone. Your parents and your larger family will always be there to watch over you.

Isabella and Cameron, I truly believe that the heart of the Universe is a warm, caring, and safe place, with a Heartbeat of Love, and big enough for all people everywhere in the world, whatever their age, or religion, or nationality.

A long time ago there was another baby like you born into the world, a person in whom people could see God so clearly that God's love and goodness just spread out everywhere he went. That baby's name was "Jesus" (which means "The Lord Saves"). Jesus grew up to be an adult just like you will. A lot of people believed that when they met Jesus, they were meeting God.

Well, Jesus is still alive in our hearts. And Jesus wants to be your very best friend. Jesus told us to "fear not, for I am with you," and that "God has not given us a spirit of cowardice and fear, but of power, love, and a sound mind." So we don't have to let those bullies and bogeymen tell us what to do—whether we meet them here in our own country, or far away in other parts of the world.

God loves each of us, all over the world, even more than we love each other. Nothing we could ever do will ever stop God from loving us. God is for us, and for everyone everywhere. God is also against everything that any of us does that hurts people. There is a moral order of right and wrong, of good and evil in the world which is above every person's and every country's particular interest and identity. But that foundation for our lives and our world is only one generation away from collapse. And you are a part of that generation. You and your friends will determine the future of the world.

Hate only creates hate. "We must not respond to our enemy in kind. We must not seek to avenge the death of innocent Americans by the death of innocent victims elsewhere, lest we become what we abhor. . . What we will do is build [forceful and effective] coalitions with other nations . . . [and] see that justice is done—but by the force of law only, never by the law of force."[123]

When you get older, your teachers and coaches will tell you that your team can only win when each of you play "one for all and all for one." It's like that with nations. When they talk about the war in Iraq, you and I have to remember as children of God that war is never between strangers, between "us" and "them," but always between brothers and sisters within the same human family.

Little ones, you don't know how very lucky you are to have been born and grow up in America. This is a great country and it wasn't made so by angry, fearful people. It was made so by free people who can be trusted to make the right choices for themselves and the freedoms they enjoy here. Your parents, grandparents, great grandparents, and people of goodwill in churches, temples, and mosques like ours across the nation have a sacred duty to leave this wonderful country in better shape than we found it . . . certainly better than it is right now. We still have a long way to go, and we're not getting any younger. That's why it will be up to you.

You are God's children, Isabella and Cameron, in whom God is well-pleased. God has given you to us and to the world because we need you to guide us into a better future.

> *"With all its sham, drudgery, and broken dreams,*
> *it is still a beautiful world.*
> *Be cheerful. Strive to be happy."*[124]

God bless you both. And may God bless the world through you.

All our Love,
Gramma Bev and Pappa Gary

"Nothing happens…But first a dream."
—CARL SANDBURG

"The future belongs to those
who believe in the beauty of their dreams."
—ELEANOR ROOSEVELT

A SONG FOR ALL THE NATIONS
AND ALL THE FAITHS

"THIS IS MY SONG"
[Tune: "Finlandia"]

This is my song, Oh God of all the nations,
A song of peace for lands afar and mine.
This is my home, the country where my heart is;
Here are my hopes, my dreams, my sacred shrine.
But other hearts in other lands are beating.
With hopes and dreams as true and high as mine.

My country's skies are bluer than the ocean,
And sunlight beams on cloverleaf and pine.
But other lands have sunlight too and clover,
And skies are everywhere as blue as mine.
Oh hear my song, oh God of all the nations,
A song of peace for their land and for mine.

May truth and freedom come to every nation.
May peace abound where strife has raged so long;
That each may seek to love and build together,
A world united, righting every wrong.
A world united in its love for freedom,
Proclaiming peace together in one song."

New Century (UCC) Hymnal #591
Words by Lloyd Stone, 1934 (verses 1 and 2)—Georgia Harkness (verse 3)
Nice harmonica/video version:
http://www.youtube.com/watch?v=LW-zWiOiCA

NOTES

FORWARD
1. Gary A. Wilburn, *The God I Don't Believe In: Charting a New Course for Christianity* (Stamford, CT: ProgressivePub, 2007).
2. Christopher Reeve, "Reeve Can't Sway Senate Foes of Stem-Cell Research" by Lauran Neergaard, The Associated Press; *Seattle Times*, April 27, 2000.
3. President-elect Barack Obama, "Speech to the Nation," January 3, 2009.

UNDIMMED BY HUMAN TEARS
4. Alexander Solzhenitsyn, "One Word of Truth...": The Nobel Lecture on Literature (London: The Bodley Head, 1978), p. 8.
5. Solzhenitsyn, *The Gulag Archipelago*, Volume II, p. 615.
6. Joan D. Chittister, O.S.B., *The Psalms: Meditations for Every Day of the Year* (New York: Crossroad Publishing Company, 1996), p. 44.
7. Jurgen Moltman, *In The End—The Beginning: The Life of Hope* (Minneapolis: Fortress Press, 2004), p. ix.
8. Ibid., pp. 90-91 (citing Isaiah 26:10).
9. Robert F. Kennedy, "Day of Affirmation," address at the University of Capetown, South Africa, June 6, 1966.—*Congressional Record*, Volume 112, p. 12430.
10. Tom Stella, *A Faith Worth Believing: Finding New Life Beyond the Rules of Religion* (San Francisco: Harper Collins, 2004), p. 108.

TAKE COURAGE
11. Thomas Paine, "The Crisis," no. 1, *The Writings of Thomas Paine (1894)*, ed. Moncure D. Conway, Vol. 1, p. 176.
12. Ryan LaMothe, St. Meinrad School of Theology, "Lectionary Homiletics," Vol. XVIII, Number 1, December 2006, p. 7.
13. William Sloane Coffin, *Credo* (Louisville: John Knox Press, 2004), p. 150.
14. Hugh Thomson Kerr, "God of the Coming Years."

LIVING ABOVE OUR CIRCUMSTANCES
15. Bree Fowler, "Civil Rights Pioneer Rosa Parks, 92, Dies", Associated Press, October 25, 2005.

16. Cassandra Spratling, "Rosa Parks, Civil Rights Heroine, Is Dead", *Free Press*, October 24, 2005.
17. William Sloane Coffin, *Credo*, op.cit., p. 120.
18. Ibid., p. 141.

TINY RIPLES OF HOPE
19. William Sloane Coffin, "Sermons from Riverside Church," Christmas, 1980.
20. Victor Landa, "We Should Talk About Poverty," *San Antonio Express-News*, 2005.
21. Alan Cowell, "A Scotsman Wields a Not-So-Invisible Hand in Africa," *The New York Times International*, Saturday, December 10, 2005, p. A4.
22. Robert F. Kennedy, "Day of Affirmation Address," University of Cape Town, Cape Town, South Africa, June 6, 1966.

WHATEVER HAPPENED TO JOHNNY?
23. Robert McAfee Brown, *Unexpected News: Reading the Bible with Third World Eyes* (Philadelphia: Westminster Press, 1984), pp. 115-116.
24. David K. Shipler, *The Working Poor: Invisible in America* (New York: Alfred A. Knopf, 2004), pp. 3-4.
25. Ibid., pp. 299-300.
26. Proverbs 14:31.

GHANDHI'S SEVEN DEADLY SOCIAL SINS
27. William Sloane Coffin, *Credo*, op.cit., pp. 9, 35.
28. Stephen R. Covey, *Principle-Centered Leadership* (London: Simon & Schuster Ltd., 1990), extract, p. 1.
29. Marty Jezer, "The Spiritual Politics of Martin Luther King, Jr." www.alter-net.org/story/14960, January 16, 2003, p. 3.
30. Stephen R. Covey, op. cit., p. 2.
31. Ibid.
32. Robert Jensen, "Best We Get Comfortable with King the Radical, Too" (*Houston Chronicle*, January 14, 2001, p. 5-C and *Fort Worth Star-Telegram*, January 15, 2000).
33. Stephen R. Covey, op. cit., p. 4.
34. Ibid., pp. 3, 4.
35. Ibid., p. 5.

GET OVER IT . . . GET ON WITH IT!
36. Jim Bishop, *F.D.R.'s Last Year: April 1944 – April 1945* (New York, NY: Pocket Books, 1975), pp. 806-807.
37. C.S. Lewis, cited by Jenny Schroedel, "Getting Unstuck: Stepping Toward Your Dreams," www.boundless.org.
38. Stephen Pressfield, *The War of Art*, cited by Jenny Schroedel, op. cit.

39. Marcus Borg and N.T. Wright, *The Meaning of Jesus: Two Visions* (New York, NY: HarperCollins Publishers, 1999), p. 8.
40. William Blake, excerpt from "Selections from Milton" in *Selected Poetry and Prose of William Blake* (New York, NY: Random House, 1953), pp. 244-245.

HOPE RISING FROM THE ASHES
41. "The Whole World Watches—and Reacts—to L.A. Riots," *Los Angeles Times* (May 5, 1992), p. H2.
42. Bettina Boxall and Vicki Torres, "Preachers Urge Worshippers to Improve Society," *Los Angeles Times* (May 9, 1992), p. A1.
43. Martin Luther King, Jr., "Where Do We Go From Here: Chaos or Community?," *A Testament of Hope: The Essential Writings of Martin Luther King, Jr.*, edited by James M. Washington (San Francisco: Harper and Row, 1986), p. 623.
44. Jessie Jackson, "A Terrible Rainbow of Protest," *Los Angeles Times* (May 4, 1992), p. B7.
45. Jeremiah 29:11.

HOPE FOR ECONOMIC JUSTICE
46. Julianne Malveaux, "How Can We Fight Poverty?" *The Advocate*, March 11, 2007, p. A17.
47. "Stories About Economic Justice," Christian Alliance For Progress, www.christianalliance.org.
48. Victor Landa, "We Should Talk About Poverty," *San Antonio Express-News*, 2005.
49. Krister Stendahl, cited by Letty M. Russell, *The Christian Century*, January 22, 1992, p. 65.
50. Ronald Nash, Poverty and Wealth, cited by *Integer* (National Foundation for the Study of Religion and Economics), Summer/Fall, 1987, p. 5.
51. William Sloane Coffin, *Credo*, op. cit., p. 61.
52. Vince Isner, "A Faithful State of The Union Address," www.FaithfulAmerica.org, 2006.
53. Jesus, Matthew 25:40.

HOPE FOR THE ENVIRONMENT
54. Andrew C. Revkin, "U.S. Predicting Steady Increase for Emissions," *The New York Times*, March 3, 2007, p.1.
55. John Hellprin, Associated Press, *The Advocate*, March 4, 2007, p. A13.
56. Sir John Houghton, cited in "The Rising Tide," *The Christian Century*, February 20, 2007, p.5.
57. Elisabeth Rosenthal and Andrew C. Revkin, "Science Panel Says Global Warming is Unequivocal," *The New York Times*, February 3, 2007, p. 1.
58. Psalm 24:1; 19:1.
59. William Sloane Coffin, *A Passion for the Possible: A Message to U.S. Churches*

(Louisville: Westminster/John Knox Press, 1993), pp. 27-29.

60. Luke 12:48.

61. The Christian Alliance for Progress: The Movement to Reclaim Christianity and Transform American Politics, www.christianalliance.org.

62. Bill McKibben, "Meltdown: Running out of time on global warming," *Christian Century*, February 20, 2007, p. 22.

63. Jim Polson, Bloomberg News, *The Advocate*, January 24, 2007, p. A11.

64. Coffin, *A Passion for the Possible: A Message to U.S. Churches*, op. cit., p. 13.

HOPE FOR THE END OF NUCLEAR WEAPONS

65. Andrew Calabrese, "Virtual Nonviolence? Civil Disobedience and Political Violence in the Information Age," *Emerald Research Register* (Emerald Group Publishing Limited, 2004), Volume 6, Number 5, p. 326.

66. Zechariah 9:9-10.

67. Hudson Stoddard, "Reflections on the New Canaan Coalition For Nuclear Arms Control, 1981-1991," May 5, 2002, New Canaan Historical Society.

68. Peter Smith, "End to Nuclear Weapons Urged: McNamara Wants Churches to Act," *The Courier-Journal*, Louisville, KY., November 12, 2005.

69. Luke 23:31.

70. Cora Weiss, "Time to Change Our Way of Thinking and Doing—a Program for Riverside for the New Century," The Riverside Church 20th Anniversary of the Disarmament Program, May 24, 1998.

71. William Sloane Coffin, "Nukes Forever? The Case for Their Abolition," sermon preached at The Riverside Church, New York City, NY, May 24, 1998.

72. Reinhold Niebuhr, cited by Kermit D. Johnson, "The Sovereign God and 'the Signs of the Times,'" *The Christian Century*, August 17-24, 1983, p. 740.

73. George P. Schultz, William J. Perry, Henry A. Kissinger and Sam Nunn, "A World Free of Nuclear Weapons," *The Wall Street Journal*, January 4, 2007, p. 15.

74. Sam Nunn, cited by Michael Crowley, "The Stuff Sam Nunn's Nightmares Are Made Of," *The New York Times Magazine*, February 25, 2007, p. 52.

75. Resources for presidential positions and statements:
   • President Eisenhower, in his "Atoms for Peace" address to the United Nations in 1953, pledged America's determination to help solve the fearful atomic dilemma—and called on the superpowers to "begin to diminish the potential destructive power of the world's atomic stockpiles."
   • President Kennedy, in the fall of 1961, warned that "mankind must put an end to war, or war will put an end to mankind. The risks in disarmament pale in comparison to the risks inherent in an unlimited arms race."
   • President Johnson, when he signed the Non-Proliferation of Nuclear Weapons Treaty in 1968, pledged that Washington and Moscow would

"pursue negotiations in good faith for the cessation of the nuclear arms race."

- President Nixon, in 1970, said that "the nuclear era places on the two preponderant powers a unique responsibility to explore means of limiting military competition."
- President Carter, in his Inaugural Address, expressed the hope that "nuclear weapons would be rid from the face of the earth."
- President Reagan called for the abolishment of "all nuclear weapons," which he considered to be "totally irrational, totally inhumane, good for nothing but killing, [and] possibly destructive of life on earth and civilization."
- President George H. Bush spoke of the need to reduce tactical nuclear weapons. President Clinton worked for a Chemical, Biological and Nuclear Weapons reduction. President George W. Bush has said that the primary challenge of future administrations is to stop nuclear proliferation and the use of weapons of mass destruction.

76. James R. Lowell, "Once to Every Man and Nation," *Boston Courier,* December 11, 1845. A poem written protesting America's war with Mexico.

HOPE FOR THE END OF TERRORISM

77. This account relies on Terry McDermot, *Perfect Soldiers: The Hijackers: Who They Were, Why They Did It* (New York: Harper Collins, 2005), pp. 231-234.
78. Louise Richardson, *What Terrorists Want: Understanding the Enemy, Containing the Threat* (New York: Random House, 2006), p. 20.
79. Ibid., pp. 24, 25.
80. Charles Kimball, *When Religion Becomes Evil* (San Francisco: HarperSanFrancisco, 2002), Chapters 1-6.
81. Richardson, op. cit., p. 41.
82. Ibid., p. 199.
83. Edward LeRoy Long, Jr., *Facing Terrorism: Responding as Christians* (Louisville: Westminster John Knox Press, 2004), pp. 94-96.
84. John Shelby Spong, "When Will We Ever Learn?" *A New Christianity for a New World,* May 28, 2003, support@johnshelbyspong.com.
85. Matthew 9:36.
86. William Sloane Coffin, *Nation,* January 12/19, 2004.

TO SEEK A NEWER WORLD

87. Peter Carlson, "Panic, Patriotism and Politics: How America Went to War 60 Years Ago," *Washington Post* editorial, reprinted in *The Advocate,* December 7, 2001.
88. I allude here to an editorial in *Christian Century* on December 17, 1941, "An Unnecessary Necessity." The author expresses a common position of mainline American Christianity during World War II. Can be read in full on the web: http://www.christiancentury.org/history.html.

89. "Deny Them Their Victory: A Religious Response to Terrorism," sponsored by the National Council of Churches and Sojourners, *The New York Times*, November 19, 2001, p. F5.

THE MYSTIC CORDS OF MEMORY
90. Alexander Smith.
91. T.S. Eliot, "Four Quartets: Burnt Norton II".
92. R. Buckminster Fuller.
93. Dwight D. Eisenhower, Radio & Television Broadcast with Prime Minister Harold Macmillan, London, August 31, 1959, cited in *Public Papers of the Presidents of the United States: Dwight D. Eisenhower* (1959), p. 625.
94. Attributed to Alexis de Tocqueville "Democracy in America" in Sherwood Eddy, *The Kingdom of God and the American Dream* (1941), Chap. 1, p. 6.
95. Carl Sandburg, interview with Frederick Van Ryn, *This Week Magazine*, January 4, 1953, p. ll.
96. Rudyard Kipling, "Recessional."

DARE WE HOPE AGAIN?
97. James Carroll, *The Boston Globe*, December 29, 2008.
98. Senator Barack Obama, Keynote Address, 2004 Democratic National Convention, Boston, MA, July 27, 2004.
99. Carroll, op. cit.
100. Barack Obama, President-Elect of the United States of America, Acceptance Speech, Grants Park, Chicago, IL, November 4, 2008.
101. Barack Obama, President of the United States of America, Inaugural Address, Washington, D.C., January 20, 2009.
102. James Baldwin, in *Healing Words*, by Caren Goldman, (New York: Marlowe & Co., 2001).

HOPE SRINGS ETERNAL
103. Peter J. Gomes, "Life Conquers All," *Yet More Sundays at Harvard: Sermons for An Academic Year* (Cambridge, MA: The Memorial Church, Harvard University, 1997), pp. 155-156.
104. A. B. Simpson.
105. Alexander Pope (1688-1744), "Essay on Man," Epistle i. Line 95.
106. Luke 24:5.
107. "At the Workbench: Easter Sunday," William L. Dols, Editor, Vol. 9, Issue 3, pp. 114-116.
108. Gerald May, "For They Shall be Comforted," in *Shalem News*, date unknown.
109. The Fetchet Family, "Memorial Foundation to Honor World Trade Center Victim," *The New Canaan Advertiser*, October 25, 2001, p. 7A.

110. William Sloane Coffin, "Our Resurrection, Too," a sermon preached on March 26, 1978, *The Riverside Preachers: Fosdick, McCracken, Campbell, Coffin*, Paul H. Sherry, editor (New York: Pilgrim Press, 1978), pp. 160, 161.

THE BEST OF MY DAYS

111. William Wordsworth.
112. Barbara Hurd, *Stirring the Mud* (New York: Houghton Mifflin, 2003), p. 109-110.
113. Reported by Jane E. Brody, "World Enough and Time for 'a Good Death,'" *The New York Times*, Tuesday, October 31, 2006, p. F8.
114. Dr. Elisabeth Kubler-Ross, On Death and Dying.
115. Forrest Church, "What I Believe," sermon preached on October 8, 2006, at All Souls Unitarian Universalist Church, New York City, NY.
116. Henri Nouwen, *Beyond the Mirror: Reflections on Death & Dying* (New York: Crossroads Publishing Company, 1990).

I WILL NOT DIE AN UNLIVED LIFE

117. Dawna Markova, *I Will Not Die An Unlived Life* (Berkeley, CA: Conari Press, 2000), pp. 128-130.
118. Ibid., p. 1-4.
119. Ibid., p. 22.
120. John 10:10.
121. Thomas Campbell, Scottish poet (1777-1844).

EPILOGUE

122. Leslie D. Weatherhead.
123. William Sloane Coffin, *Nation*, January 12-19, 2004.
124. "Desiderata", written by Max Ehrmann in the 1920's—not "Found in Old St. Paul's Church in 1692"!

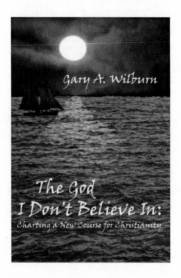